HONORING THE
PRIESTHOOD
AS A DEACON, A TEACHER, AND A PRIEST

JOHN BYTHEWAY

DESERET BOOK
SALT LAKE CITY, UTAH

Cover photo by Alan Blakely

Illustrations on pages 11, 21, 30, 40, 54, 72, 105, 111, 121, and 141 by Nathan Pinnock

First printing in hardbound 2002
First printing in paperbound 2008

Visit us at DeseretBook.com

Library of Congress Cataloging-in-Publication Data

Bytheway, John, 1962-
    Honoring the priesthood as a deacon, a teacher, and a priest /John Bytheway.
      p. cm.
    Summary: Offers advice to members of the Aaronic Priesthood of the Mormon Church on how to conduct themselves properly. Includes bibliographical references and index.
    ISBN-10 1-57008-863-2 (hardbound : alk. paper)
    ISBN-13 978-1-57008-863-6 (hardbound : alk. paper)
    ISBN-13 978-1-59038-876-1 (paperbound)
    1. Aaronic Priesthood (Mormon Church) 2. Mormon youth—
Religious life.   [1. Aaronic Priesthood (Mormon Church)
2. Mormons—Religious life. 3. Conduct of life.]   I. Title.
    BX8659.5B98 2002
    248.8'32'088283—dc21   2002011086

Printed in the United States of America
R. R. Donnelley and Sons, Crawfordsville, IN

10   9   8   7   6   5   4   3   2   1

HONORING THE

PRIESTHOOD

AS A DEACON, A TEACHER, AND A PRIEST

BOOKS

Are Your Standards Fences or Guardrails?
A Crash Course in Teenage Survival
How to Be an Extraordinary Missionary
How to Be an Extraordinary Teenager
How to Be Totally Miserable
Isaiah for Airheads
Righteous Warriors: Lessons from the War Chapters in the Book of Mormon
What I Wish I'd Known Before My Mission
What I Wish I'd Known When I Was Single
You're Gonna Make It through Junior High

AUDIO

The Best Three Hours of the Week
Bytheway, It's John: The Second Verse
First Solo: Learning to Recognize the Spirit
Five Scriptures That Will Help You Get through Almost Anything
Get an Attitude: Heroic Examples from the Book of Mormon
Honoring the Priesthood As a Deacon, a Teacher, and a Priest
How to Be an Extraordinary Missionary
How to Be an Extraordinary Teenager
How to Be Totally Miserable/SOS
No-Brainers: 5 Hard Decisions That the Gospel Makes Easy
Righteous Warriors: Lessons from the War Chapters in the Book of Mormon
Rough Start, Great Finish
The Tour de Family: Doing Your Part to Help Your Family Succeed
Turn Off the TV and Get a Life!
What Are You Carrying in Your Backpack?
What I Wish I'd Known Before My Mission
What I Wish I'd Known When I Was Single
Whose Values Do You Value?

DVD

The Best Three Hours of the Week
Heroes: Lessons from the Book of Mormon
Standards Night Live
What's in Your Backpack?

Contents

I. THE PRIESTHOOD

II. OUTWARD ORDINANCES

III. HONORING YOUR PRIESTHOOD

IV. PREPARING FOR THE MELCHIZEDEK PRIESTHOOD

Acknowledgments

I'd like to thank a number of young men in the Aaronic Priesthood who read the manuscript and helped me put this book together—Layne Christensen II, Taylor Curtis, Drew Francis, Christian Loveridge, and Kevin Wilder.

Thanks also to my respected friends David Hyde, for allowing me to share one of his stories; Brad Wilcox, for the excerpts from his book; and Kim Peterson, for his insights on the sacrament. As always, I am indebted to the publishing department at Deseret Book, especially Michael Morris and Shauna Gibby. I am also grateful to Nathan Pinnock for his fine illustrations and for his friendship.

Finally, thanks to my wife, Kimberly, for her continued support and valuable insights.

A Note

This book was written to be read from start to finish whether you're a deacon, teacher, or priest. Some chapters are a little longer than others, but I expect that as your responsibilities in the priesthood increase, your attention span will too.

You Are Not Normal

Most people say that teenage boys don't read books. Obviously, they have never met you.

This book was written for some of the finest young men in the world, which is why there's a copy in *your* hands. Maybe ordinary young men don't read books, but you, my friend, are not ordinary.

Impressive new deacons are reading this book because they want to know what deacons do, and how their responsibilities will change when they get older. Exceptional teachers are reading because they want to know what's expected of them, and how they can be an example to other teachers in their quorum and to deacons in their ward. Extraordinary priests are reading because they want to know how to honor their priesthood and prepare for their next major step—receiving the Melchizedek Priesthood.

Whichever one you are—deacon, teacher, or priest—I honor you as much as I honor the president of the United States. Maybe even more. Does that sound strange? Good. Keep reading.

You young men, you are a royal priesthood. Do you ever pause to think of the wonder of it? You have had hands placed upon your heads to receive that same priesthood exercised by John who baptized Jesus of Nazareth. With worthiness in your lives, you may enjoy the comforting, protecting, guiding influence of ministering angels. No individual of earthly royalty has a blessing as great. Live for it. Be worthy of it, is my plea to each of you (Gordon B. Hinckley, Teachings of Gordon B. Hinckley *[Salt Lake City: Deseret Book, 1997], 485).*

1

Congratulations, You Have the Priesthood!

Imagine what it would be like to be the president of the United States? As the president, you get to

- Travel the world.
- Lead a superpower.
- Fly in your own 747.

Well-armed men in dark suits and sunglasses protect you wherever you go. Every time you open your mouth, cameras flash and TV cameras roll. You can be on the news every day.

Sound like fun? I'm sure it is—on some days. But you, as a very young man, have an opportunity to be something even more significant than the president. You can be a *deacon.*

Early in the last century, a man named Reed Smoot achieved quite a bit in politics. In fact, Senator Smoot was offered the Republican nomination to become the president of the United States—twice. There was just one condition: He had to deny his religion. You see, Brother Smoot was a Latter-day Saint.

A friend asked him, "Wouldn't it be worth it?" Brother Smoot whirled around, took him by the arm, and said, "Young man, maybe you do not know my stand in regard to my Church. If I had to take my choice of being a deacon in the Church of Jesus Christ of Latter-day Saints, or being the President of the United States, I would be a deacon" (Bryant S. Hinckley, *The Faith of Our Pioneer Fathers* [Salt Lake City: Bookcraft, 1956], 202).

Yes, you could be the president and lead a super-power, but imagine having the power of God! The president has some power in the world, but God *made* the world! The president will eventually have to leave office, but you never will!

Elder LeGrand Richards was an apostle back when I was a deacon. One day, Elder Richards's son came home and asked, "Daddy, I have more author-ity than the President of the United States, haven't I?" Elder Richards wasn't sure what to say at first.

"It took my breath away. I had to think pretty fast, and finally I said, 'Well, yes, you do. The

President of the United States gets his authority from the people, and when his term of office expires, his authority is all gone. Yours comes from the Lord, and if you will live for it, it will be yours forever and ever'" (Conference Report, October 1967, 109).

What makes having the priesthood so important?

2

There's Something Different in the House

When I was a boy, sometimes I'd bring things home that my mother wished I hadn't—a snake or a turtle or a worm. She'd usually ask me three questions:

What is that?

Where did you get it?

What are you going to do with it?

When you receive the Aaronic Priesthood and bring it into your home, your mother will be thrilled. But if she asked you the same three questions about the priesthood, how would you answer?

WHAT IS IT?

I'm sure you've noticed the stars and planets shining in the sky on a dark night? Do you know what holds them in place? *Priesthood.* Do you know by what power they were created? *Priesthood.* And do you know what power you have? *Priesthood.*

President Brigham Young said, "The Priesthood . . . is the power by which the worlds are and were created, and the power by which they are now held in existence, and by which all that are yet to come will be organized, governed, controlled and sustained" (Preston Nibley, *Brigham Young: The Man and His Work,* 4th ed. [Salt Lake City: Deseret Book, 1960], 453).

Simply put, "the priesthood is the power and authority of God, delegated to man on earth, to act in all things for the salvation of men" (Bruce R. McConkie, "The Ten Bles-sings of the Priesthood," *Ensign,* November 1977, 33). We use the priesthood to do the Lord's work on earth while the Lord uses it for all kinds of things on earth *and* in heaven—including holding the universe together.

Priesthood is different from other kinds of authority. For example, when you get your driver's license, you'll have authority to drive a car. If you drive too fast or run a red light, you'll still have your license, or your authority to drive—as long as the police don't notice. Priesthood power, however, is different. If you abuse it, you lose it. The Lord sees *everything* we do, and our priesthood authority can be withdrawn if we don't honor it (D&C 121:36–37).

WHERE DID YOU GET IT?

You got your priesthood from the person who ordained you, but it goes back a lot further than that. In 1829, when Joseph Smith and Oliver Cowdery were translating the Book of Mormon, they noticed something about baptism, and they wondered if they were supposed to be baptized. So Joseph and Oliver went into the woods to pray about it.

John the Baptist, the same person who baptized Jesus, appeared and ordained them to the Aaronic Priesthood. Then he instructed them to baptize each other. Joseph Smith recorded this whole miraculous event rather calmly (JS–H 1:68–71), but Oliver Cowdery was beside himself with excitement. Sometimes young people don't notice very much excitement in the church. You want excitement? Count the exclamation points (!) in the next few paragraphs.

What joy! what wonder! what amazement! . . . His voice, though mild, pierced to the center, and his words, "I am thy fellow-servant," dispelled every fear. We listened, we gazed, we admired! . . . Where was room for doubt? Nowhere; uncertainty had fled, doubt had sunk no more to rise, while fiction and deception had fled forever!

But, dear brother, think, further think for a moment, what joy filled our hearts, and with what surprise we must have bowed, (for who would not have bowed the knee for such a blessing?) when we received under his hand the Holy Priesthood as he said, "Upon you my fellow-servants, in the name of Messiah, I confer this Priesthood and this authority, which shall remain upon earth, that the Sons of Levi may yet offer an offering unto the Lord in righteousness!"

I shall not attempt to paint to you the feelings of this heart, nor the majestic beauty and glory which surrounded us on this occasion; but you will believe me when I say, that earth, nor men, with the eloquence of time, cannot begin to clothe language in as interesting and sublime a manner as

this holy personage (Oliver Cowdery account, following JS–H in the Pearl of Great Price).

I count six exclamation points. Yes, Oliver was on fire with excitement, and we should be too because the priesthood was restored and we have it!

Joseph Smith and Oliver Cowdery received the Aaronic Priesthood from John the Baptist. You should ask your father or your quorum advisor about your personal "line of authority." It will show how your priesthood was passed from Jesus Christ himself all the way down to you.

You now know what priesthood is and where it came from, but what about that next question. What are you going to do with it?

WHAT ARE YOU GOING TO DO WITH IT?

You're going to serve, that's what. We use the priesthood to make others' lives better. That's the Lord's work on earth. When you think of the purpose of the priesthood, just remember the song "Serve," and then think of the next word: "Serve Him" (Hymns, 1985, no. 249). The ___ od is to serve each other (Mosiah ___ hat priesthood is all about.

The president of the Aaronic Priesthood in your ward is the bishop (if you're in a branch, it's the branch president). You take your orders from him. Our prophet is the president of the Church. We might say he is the "head" of the Church on earth. If that's true, then who are the legs of the Church? The deacons are. In President Young's day, deacons were called the "legs and feet" of the church.

A former Church historian wrote:

> Without deacon power, the Church would suffer in two ways. First, bishops and others would have to drop some of their own duties in order to take upon themselves the work that deacons are supposed to do. Second, and perhaps most important, if a generation of deacons fail, within two years there would be no teachers, in four years no priests, and after a decade or two the ranks of the Melchizedek Priesthood quorums would not be filled with the prepared and qualified adults, graduates of the preparatory Aaronic Priesthood (William G. Hartley, "Deacon Power," in *Priesthood in Action* [Salt Lake City: New Era, 1986], 72).

(So next time you go to an activity, and you see all the young men running around, just nod your head and say, "Yup. We're the legs of the Church.")

A big part of what you do with the priesthood is to help in performing ordinances. The Lord said that the Aaronic Priesthood "is an appendage to the greater, or the Melchizedek Priesthood, and has power in administering outward ordinances" (D&C 107:14). An "appendage" is a part of something greater. "Outward ordinances" are those done out in the open—physical things we can all see. They include things like baptism and administration of the sacrament, both of which are Aaronic Priesthood ordinances. We'll read about ordinances next.

AMAZING YOUNG MEN FROM THE PAST

PRE-DEACON AGE:

Noah was ten years old when he received the priesthood (D&C 107:52).

Mormon was ten years old when Ammoron charged him to observe the doings of the people in preparation for completing the Book of Mormon record (Mormon 1:2–4).

DEACON AGE:

Jesus was twelve years old when he spoke to the doctors in the temple and answered their questions (JST, Luke 2:46).

Anthon H. Lund was called on a mission when he was thirteen years old. He later served twenty years in the First Presidency.

TEACHER AGE:

Mormon was fifteen when he was "visited of the Lord" (Mormon 1:15). That same year he was appointed to lead the armies of the Nephites (Mormon 2:2).

Joseph Smith was fourteen when he received the First Vision (JS–H 1:7).

Joseph F. Smith was fifteen when he was went on a mission to Hawaii.

PRIEST AGE:

Joseph the son of Jacob was seventeen when he received the coat of many colors (Genesis 37:2).

Joseph Smith was seventeen years old when he was visited by Moroni.

Matthew Cowley was called to be a missionary at seventeen. He later served as an apostle.

UNKNOWN AGES:

The two thousand stripling warriors, who were "very young" (Alma 56:46).

Daniel, Shadrach, Meshach, and Abednego, who refused to worship the idols of King Nebuchadnezzar (Daniel 1–3).

Samuel, who was a child when he heard the voice of the Lord as he lay down to sleep (1 Samuel 3).

The two ordinances most directly related to the atonement of Jesus Christ are Aaronic Priesthood ordinances—the sacrament and baptism (Elder Robert L. Backman, "They Were Awesome," in Priesthood in Action *[Salt Lake City, New Era, 1986], 60).*

II. OUTWARD ORDINANCES

3

The Outward Ordinance of Baptism

Although he was old, and his voice quivered, his speech was powerful and compelling. Everyone who heard him found it impossible to disagree! His eyes were fixed and his fists clenched. No one tried to stop him, because no one dared try. The corrupt judges could rebel in their hearts, but they had to listen. Finally the prophet in chains finished his rebuke. His final words echoed in the judgment hall, and for nearly a minute no one made a sound until a single voice broke the silence.

"I plead with you, do not be angry with this man!" a youthful judge shouted. "He has spoken the truth concerning our iniquities! I plead with you to let him depart in peace!" All eyes turned immediately to the young man, and then to the king. What would he do? The King's face grew red with anger. Slowly he lifted

his gaze from the floor, and with the raise of his right hand, summoned the guards to cast the judge out.

The young man struggled to speak again, but the guards overpowered him and threw him out of the chamber into the hall. His footsteps could be heard as he ran away.

The king paused for a moment then looked again to the guards and pronounced a death sentence on the fleeing judge. "Slay him." With a gesture of salute, they turned and disappeared in pursuit.

You've heard this story before. In fact you've seen a famous painting depicting this dramatic event. The prophet, of course, was Abinadi, the wicked king was Noah, and the young judge was Alma the Elder (Mosiah 13–17). Alma was the only one who believed the prophet Abinadi, and as far as we know, Abinadi never knew that Alma escaped with his life. It's possible that he may have gone to his death feeling "that he failed as a missionary" (Joseph B. Wirthlin, *Finding Peace in Our Lives* [Salt Lake City: Deseret Book, 1995], 220).

What's the rest of the story? Today we know that Abinadi did not fail! After Alma made his escape, he hid himself and recorded the final sermon of the prophet Abinadi. Later, Alma returned to the city and taught the people in secret. Eventually, he led his followers to the waters of Mormon to be baptized.

As a new priest (or deacon or teacher who is preparing to become a priest), you may never have to go through such a dangerous ordeal in preparation to perform a baptism. But you will find that any baptism you perform is an exciting adventure.

Baptism is one of the outward ordinances performed by those who hold the Aaronic Priesthood. At the water's edge, Alma gave those who believed the words of Abinadi what Elder Jeffrey R. Holland has called "the most complete scriptural statement on record as to what the newly baptized commit to do and be" (*Christ and the New Covenant* [Salt Lake City: Deseret Book, 1997], 106). By being baptized, we commit to:

- Come into the fold of God.
- Be called God's people.
- Bear one another's burdens.
- Mourn with those who mourn.
- Comfort those who stand in need of comfort.

Stand as witnesses of God at all times, in all things, and in all places.

Serve God and keep his commandments (Mosiah 18:8–10).

Baptism is a symbol. Symbols were very important to ancient people, and they're important today.

Every time you sit down at the computer, you use symbols. A computer game is represented by an icon or a symbol on your computer monitor. If you move the arrow to the icon and double click your mouse, the program begins. In the same way, a symbol is a representation of something else.

THE SYMBOL OF BAPTISM

Have you ever noticed that baptismal fonts are always below ground level? In the temple, where we perform baptisms for the dead, the font is always in the basement. Why? Because in baptism, we are "buried" in the water, and then we come up out of the water and are "born again." Being baptized is like being buried in the ground, and then being resurrected and coming up out of the ground! That's why baptismal fonts are below ground level.

The apostle Paul said, "Therefore we are buried with him by baptism into death: that like as Christ was raised up from the dead by the glory of the Father, even so we also should walk in newness of life" (Romans 6:4). In other words, we bury the "old man of sin" and are born again as new creatures to a new way of life.

When a baby is inside its mother, it is completely surrounded by water, or, to use the medical term, "amniotic fluid." When we're "born again," or baptized, we're also immersed, or surrounded by water.

The symbol of baptism is so important that not only was Jesus baptized but also the entire earth itself was baptized when the Lord sent the Flood. Eventually, the earth will be "baptized with fire" and then resurrected! You may have heard it put this way: "The earth will be renewed and receive its paradisiacal glory" (A of F 1:10).

Part of the ordinance of baptism and confirmation is that we receive a remission of our sins. Everyone is grateful for the ordinance of baptism because we have our sins taken away and we get to start all over again with a clean slate! Wouldn't it be nice if we could be baptized every week? You know what? We can.

4

Being Baptized Again by Partaking of the Sacrament

Do you remember the feeling you had when you were baptized—that sweet, clean feeling of a pure soul, having been forgiven, washed clean through the merits of the Savior? If we partake of the sacrament worthily, we can feel that way regularly, for we renew that covenant, which includes his forgiveness (John H. Groberg, "The Beauty and Importance of the Sacrament," Ensign, *May 1989, 38).*

No man goes away from this Church and becomes an apostate in a week, nor in a month. It is a slow process. The one thing that would make for the safety of every man and woman would be to appear at the sacrament table every Sabbath day. . . . The road to the sacrament table is the path of safety for Latter-day Saints (Melvin J. Ballard, "The Sacramental Covenant," Improvement Era, *October 1919, 1025–31).*

When we partake of the sacrament worthily, it is as if we were baptized all over again. What a privilege! What an opportunity!

The sacrament is another outward ordinance in which all offices of the Aaronic priesthood participate. The bishop presides, the priests bless, the teachers prepare, and the deacons pass. The sacrament of the Lord's Supper, or "the sacrament" for short, is a chance for all members of the Church to renew the covenants they made at baptism, and it is full of beautiful and interesting symbols.

I wish someone had sat me down and told me about the sacrament symbols when I was a deacon. Maybe they tried to and I wasn't listening. I learned most of what I know about the sacrament *after* my mission. In fact, when you're done reading this chapter, you will know more about the sacrament as a teenager than I did as a returned missionary!

Before sacrament meeting starts, members of the teacher's quorum go to the chapel. First they put a cloth on the sacrament table. Then they go to the sacrament preparation room, where they fill the trays with bread and the cups with water. Let's look at some of the symbols:

The table. The sacrament table is like the table at which Jesus gave his disciples the Last Supper. Just like those disciples, we sit down in fellowship and eat with the Lord.

The sacrament table is also like an altar. An altar is where sacrifices occur, and when we use the sacrament table we remember the sacrifice Jesus made for us. In fact, one of the altars in the ancient temple was called the "table of the Lord" (Malachi 1:12; Ezekiel 41:22).

Look at the chapel in your ward building. Notice that the sacrament table is not in the back or to the side. It is in front of the chapel, where everyone can see it and be reminded of its symbolism.

The cloth. A white cloth covers the bread and water trays just like the white cloth that covered Jesus' body when he was buried in the tomb. The next time you're at church, look closely at the sacrament table and see if it doesn't resemble a body covered by a cloth. Also, read John 20:7 and notice what the resurrected Jesus did with the cloth before he left the tomb.

The hymn. A hymn is like a prayer (D&C 25:12). Once during my mission, I was talking to my companion during a hymn. My mission president leaned over to me and said, "Elder, you wouldn't talk during a prayer, would you?" After I  answered, "No," he said, "Well, the Lord said that the song of the righteous is a prayer unto me" (D&C 25:12). Needless to say, I stopped talking.

Like the disciples, who sang a hymn at the Last Supper (Matthew 26:30), we also sing a sacrament hymn. This hymn is always about the atonement of Jesus Christ.

The bread. The bread is a symbol of Jesus' body. The teachers don't break the bread in the sacrament preparation room, and we don't buy bread that is already in small pieces. During the sacrament hymn, the priests stand up at the table, pick up the bread, and then tear it into small pieces.

Jesus called himself the "bread of life." The priests tear the bread in pieces in remembrance of his body, which was "bruised, broken, torn for us" (*Hymns*, 1985, no. 181). The priests serve as a visual aid while the rest of us sing a hymn about the Atonement.

In the Old Testament, we read about a bread-like substance called *manna* that came from above and fed the children of Israel. Manna kept them alive during their wanderings. Today the sacrament reminds us that Jesus, the "bread of life," also came from above and gives us the promise of eternal life.

It's interesting to remember that the word *Bethlehem,* the place where Jesus was born, means "house of bread" (*Bible Dictionary,* 621).

Kneeling to pray. When we kneel down, it's impossible to run away. Kneeling is a posture of humility and a symbol of submitting our will to God's will. The scriptures often speak of the proud being "lifted up in the pride of [their] hearts" and wearing "stiff necks and high heads" (Jacob 2:13; 2 Nephi 26:20; Alma 4:6; Mormon 8:28). Bowing our heads is also a posture of humility and submission to God's will.

Right hand. If you had to testify in a trial, you would be required to raise your right hand and swear to tell the truth. Our right hand is our covenant-making hand. That's why, when possible, we use our right hand to take the sacrament. The sacrament helps us renew our baptismal covenants (Russell M. Nelson, "I Have a Question," *Ensign,* March 1983, 68).

Eating the bread and drinking the water. When we eat the bread, it becomes part of us. In the

same way, the sacrifice Jesus made should become a part of us and affect everything we do. Sister Ardeth Kapp told the story of a young man who was thrilled when he discovered that Sister Kapp had met the prophet. After shaking her hand, he looked at his own hand and said, "I'll never wash my hand." Sister Kapp continued:

Considering the problems this decision might cause, I suggested that he probably should wash his hand and just keep the memory in his mind. This suggestion was not acceptable. He had a better idea. "Okay," he said. "I'll wash my hand, but I'll save the water." That seemed like a good suggestion, although I supposed he was only joking.

Brent left the room. A few minutes later, he returned this time carrying a plastic bag dripping with water. Before anyone could question him, he proudly announced, "I washed my hand," holding up the bag full of water for all to see. We talked about the water in the bag and how that was a distant connection to the Prophet. . . .

After a few minutes, Brent got up and, taking his treasure with him, left the room. While I wondered if we would see him again before we left, he returned, this time without the plastic bag full of water. He had determined a better solution for his desire to be in touch with the Prophet. Standing in the doorway with his T-shirt wet all the way down the front, he explained what he had done. "I drank the water," he said (*My Neighbor, My Sister, My Friend* [Salt Lake City: Deseret Book, 1990], 180).

This story makes you smile at first, but remember what Sister Kapp said. "Just keep the memory in your mind." And what do we do each Sunday? We covenant to remember the Savior, and we don't just talk about it. We use the symbol of taking the bread and water and putting them inside of us.

Jesus shed his blood in the Garden of Gethsemane and on the cross. Because of his atonement, each of us can be cleansed from our sins. We often speak of having our garments "cleansed . . . through the blood of Christ" (Alma 5:27). Usually, we think of blood as something that would stain, but Jesus' blood is a symbol of something that cleanses.

In the early days of the restored Church, the Saints used wine for the sacrament until they were told by revelation that it didn't matter what they used, as long as they administered the sacrament to glorify God and remember Jesus' sacrifice (D&C 27:2). Today we use water. In the New Testament, Jesus called the gospel "living water" (John 4:10). With that in mind, it's interesting to note the mention of bread and water in Alma 5:34: "Yea, he saith: Come unto me and ye shall partake of the fruit of the tree of life; yea, ye shall eat and drink of the bread and the waters of life freely."

Partaking of the sacrament is something we do every week—not just during Christmas or Easter. Perhaps this is because the Lord wants to remind us of our duty every seven days, not semiannually.

DECIDE NOW TO BE VALIANT

DAVID O. MCKAY:

"O teachers, yours is an important calling! God help you to be true to it, to feel that part of the responsibility of carrying on God's work, in this the last dispensation, rests upon you" (Conference Report, October 1916, 60).

SPENCER W. KIMBALL:

"You can determine now that you will be the most faithful deacon and teacher and priest. You can decide that now with an irrevocable covenant. You can be a good student; you can use your time properly and efficiently. All the balance of your life you can be happy if you use your time well" (Conference Report, April 1974, 125).

EZRA TAFT BENSON:

"As a fourteen-year-old boy [President Spencer W. Kimball], accepted the challenge of reading the Bible from cover to cover. Most of his reading was done by coal oil light in his attic bedroom. He read every night until he completed the 1,519 pages, which took him approximately a year; but he attained his goal" (*Come, Listen to a Prophet's Voice* [Salt Lake City: Deseret Book, 1990], 2–3).

5

The Sacrament Prayers

Imagine one of your friends who doesn't know much about the Church calling you up some Saturday night and saying, "What are you doing tomorrow?" You could answer, "I'm going to Church. And with priesthood authority that I can trace in about seven steps back to Jesus Christ himself, I'm going to kneel in front of a congregation of two hundred to three hundred people and place them under a binding covenant with God. What are you going to do?"

Your friend might say, "Oh. I was just going to watch TV."

The Lord puts an amazing amount of responsibility on sixteen- to eighteen-year-old priests in our Church, doesn't he? President Gordon B. Hinckley expressed it like this:

When you, as a priest, kneel at the sacrament table and offer up the prayer, which came by revelation, you place the entire congregation under covenant with the Lord. Is this a small thing? It is a most important and remarkable thing.

Now, my dear young brethren, if we are to enjoy the ministering of angels, if we are to teach the gospel of repentance, if we are to baptize by immersion for the remission of sins, if we are to administer to the membership of the Church the emblems of the sacrifice of our Lord, then we must be worthy to do so.

You cannot consistently so serve on the Sabbath and fail to live the standards of the Church during the week. It is totally wrong for you to take the name of the Lord in vain and indulge in filthy and unseemly talk at school or at work, and then kneel at the sacrament table on Sunday. You cannot drink beer or partake of illegal drugs and be worthy of the ministering of angels. You cannot be immoral in talk or in practice and expect the Lord to honor your service in teaching repentance or baptizing for the remission of sins. As those holding His holy priesthood, you must be worthy fellow servants ("The Aaronic Priesthood—a Gift from God," *Ensign*, May 1988, 46).

THE LORD'S FAVORITE SCRIPTURE

Brother Gary L. Poll once suggested that if Heavenly Father had a favorite scripture, "he might arrange it so that his people would hear it often. He might arrange it so that the person repeating the scripture would have the priesthood, and would be kneeling; and those listening to the scripture would have their eyes closed" (*A Dozen Ideas for Teaching the Book of Mormon with Power* [Salt Lake City: The Church of Jesus Christ of Latter-day Saints, August 1997], audiocassette).

As you might have guessed, Brother Poll was suggesting that the prayers offered over the sacrament, usually by members of the Aaronic Priesthood, could be Heavenly Father's favorite scripture. In this chapter, we'll talk about the prayers phrase by phrase as we look at them a little closer.

The Blessing on the Bread

"O God, the Eternal Father." Our first article of faith states, "We believe in God, the Eternal Father, and in His Son, Jesus Christ, and in the Holy Ghost." In the sacrament prayers, we address the Eternal Father, the Father of the spirits of all men (Hebrews 12:9), and the Father of Jesus Christ, the Son of God.

"We ask thee in the name of thy Son, Jesus Christ." Jesus is our advocate with the Father. He told the Nephites, "Ye must always pray unto the Father in my name" (3 Nephi 18:19). In keeping with the Savior's instructions, we offer this prayer, and all other prayers, to our Heavenly Father, in the name of Jesus Christ.

"To bless and sanctify this bread." If you fed five thousand people a free lunch, do you think they would follow you? After Jesus fed the five thousand with loaves and fishes, many in the multitude followed him in hopes that he would feed them again. The next day, Jesus spoke to those who sought him during the night. He told them not to seek for food that perishes but for food that endures. These people didn't have refrigerators or preservatives, and they must have been excited to hear about food that never goes bad. So they said to the Savior, "Lord, evermore give us this bread. And Jesus said unto them, I am the bread of life: he that cometh to me shall never hunger; and he that believeth on me shall never thirst" (John 6:34–35).

"To the souls of all those who partake of it."
When we bless our food or refreshments, we often use the wording "to nourish and strengthen our *bodies.*" But blessing the sacrament to our souls is different. Jesus said if we ate of the bread of life, we would never hunger again! Clearly, he was talking about bread for the soul, or for the spirit and body together. The scriptures teach that "the spirit and the body are the soul of man" (D&C 88:15). Thus, the manna of the Old Testament was sent to nourish and strengthen bodies, but the bread of life of the New Testament is for the nourishment of body and spirit, or, in other words, for the soul. Jesus taught the Nephites, "He that eateth this bread eateth of my body to his soul; and he that drinketh of this wine drinketh of my blood to his soul; and his soul shall never hunger nor thirst, but shall be filled" (3 Nephi 20:8).

"That they may eat in remembrance of the body of thy Son." This portion of the sacrament prayer has meant more to me in the past few years than ever before in my life. My father has Parkinson's disease and now relies on a wife, a walker, and a wheelchair to get around. Each Sunday, when I hear the priest use the words "in

remembrance of the body of thy Son," I choose to remember the empty tomb. I'm so happy to know that Jesus was resurrected. Because he rose again, we will all rise again. Someday, I will see my earthly father with my earthly mother. He'll be standing straight and tall, with no walker and no wheelchair.

My parents always taught me that I was supposed to "think about Jesus" during the sacrament. Sometimes I wasn't sure what to think about. Today, my favorite thing to remember about Jesus' body is that it was gone when the disciples came to the tomb. In the words of the angel, "He is not here: for he is risen, as he said" (Matthew 28:6).

"And witness unto thee, O God, the Eternal Father, that they are willing to take upon them the name of thy Son." What does "take upon us" mean? Well, when you were born, your parents gave you a name. When you're *born again,* you take upon you the name of Christ. When you covenant to live the life of a disciple of Christ, it's as if you're saying, "Hey, everyone, do you want to see what Latter-day Saints are all about? Watch me. Do you want to see how we treat people? Even people who don't do us any good? Watch me. Do you want to see what kind of movies we see and how we talk and dress? Watch me." Taking upon us the name of Christ is a huge responsibility!

Perhaps taking his name upon us has another meaning as well. Look at the front cover of your scriptures. Is your name embossed there? If so, we might say that your scriptures have "taken your name upon them." What does that mean? It means those scriptures belong to you. In the same way, when we take upon us the name of Christ, we belong to him. The Lord told Alma the Elder, "Blessed is this people who are willing to bear my name; for in my name shall they be called; and they are mine" (Mosiah 26:18). It's nice to know that we are his! He has put his name on us, and we belong to him.

"And always remember him." *Remember* is a very important word. President Spencer W. Kimball taught:

> When you look in the dictionary for the most important word, do you know what it is? It could be *remember*. Because all of you have made covenants—you know what to do and you know how to do it—our greatest need is to remember. That is why everyone goes to sacrament meeting every Sabbath day—to take the sacrament and listen to the priests pray that they "may always remember him and keep his commandments which he has given them." Nobody should ever forget to go to sacrament meeting. *Remember* is the word.

Remember is the program ("Circles of Exaltation," in *Charge to Religious Educators,* 2d ed. [Salt Lake City: The Church of Jesus Christ of Latter-day Saints, 1982], 12).

It's interesting how often the Book of Mormon uses the word *remember.* It uses *remember* to describe the righteous: "Yea, they did remember how great things the Lord had done for them" (Alma 62:50). And it uses *remember* to describe the wicked: "Ye are swift to do iniquity but slow to remember the Lord your God" (1 Nephi 17:45).

Elder Gerald N. Lund once told a story I will never forget. I remember it every time I hear the priests pray. He told of a magazine article that described "belaying," a backup system rock climbers use to prevent accidents. Each climber wears a harness that is connected to his climbing partner with rope. Once a climber has ascended the rock and is secure in his position, he places special mechanical devices into the crevices and irregularities in the rock so that he can support not only his own weight but also the weight of his partner. When everything is in place, the belayer calls down to his partner, "You're on belay." Brother Lund shared this story from a magazine article about the experience of an expert climber named Czenzcush:

Belaying has brought Czenzcush his best and worst moments in mountain climbing. Czenzcush  once fell from a high precipice, yanking out three mechanical supports, and pulling his belayer off a ledge. He was stopped upside-down, ten feet from the ground when his spread-eagled belayer arrested the fall with the strength of his outstretched arms and digging his fingers into the rock. "Don saved my life," says, Czenzcush. "How do you respond to a guy like that? Do you give him a used climbing rope for Christmas? No. You just remember him. You just always remember him (Eric G. Anderson, "The Vertical Limit," *Private Practice,* November 1979, 21, as cited in Gerald N. Lund, *Helping Students Understand the Events of the Atoning Sacrifice* [Salt Lake City: The Church of Jesus Christ of Latter-day Saints, 1992], audiocassette).

The sacrament prayers remind us how we should respond to someone who stretched out his arms and saved us from the Fall. We just remember him. We just always remember him.

"And keep his commandments which he has given them." Jesus taught, "If ye love me, keep my commandments" (John 14:15). Keeping all the commandments is a pretty tall order. For mortal and fallen man, it's impossible. But that is exactly why we take the sacrament so often. Brother Stephen E. Robinson taught:

> Because conversion and repentance are not once-and-for-all events, and because we cannot keep all the commandments all the time, the covenant must be renewed and reaffirmed on a regular basis. Fallen beings like ourselves need to be reminded of the covenant we made and the commitment we expressed at baptism. We need frequent opportunities for course corrections. In many denominations, it would be thought odd that the sacrament of the Lord's Supper is offered every week. Yet Latter-day Saints know that imperfect beings must regularly reaffirm their personal goal of perfection, being justified in the meantime by the atonement of Christ.
>
> Accordingly, each week we come before the Lord as we prepare for the sacrament and say essentially, "Heavenly Father, I wasn't perfect again this week, but I repent of my sins and reaffirm my commitment to keep all the commandments. I promise to go back and try again with all my heart, might, mind,

and strength. I still want and need the cleansing that comes through faith, repentance, and baptism. Please extend my contract, my covenant of baptism, and grant me the continued blessings of the Atonement and the companionship of the Holy Ghost" (*Believing Christ: The Parable of the Bicycle and Other Good News* [Salt Lake City: Deseret Book, 1992], 52).

"That they may always have his Spirit to be with them. Amen." I can't think of anything your parents or bishop would want more for you than that the Lord's spirit always be with you. With the Lord's spirit, you will be protected and guided beyond your own abilities.

Having the Lord's spirit is perhaps the greatest blessing that comes to us as we take his name upon us and always remember him. President George Q. Cannon taught:

When we went forth into the waters of baptism and covenanted with our Father in Heaven to serve Him and keep His commandments, He bound Himself also by covenant to us that He would never desert us, never leave us to ourselves, never forget us, that in the midst of trials and hardships, when everything was arrayed against us, He would be near unto us and would sustain us (*Gospel Truth— Discourses and Writings of President George Q. Cannon,* ed. Jerreld L. Newquist, 2 vols. [Salt Lake City: Deseret Book, 1974], 1:170).

If the Lord asks us to always remember him, we can be sure that because he is perfect, he *always* remembers us. "Yea, they may forget, yet will I not forget thee, O house of Israel. Behold, I have graven thee upon the palms of my hands" (1 Nephi 21:15–16). It's nice to know that he always remembers us, and wants us to remember him, so that we can have his spirit with us.

The Blessing on the Water

The prayer over the water is similar to the prayer over the bread in that it addresses the Eternal Father in the name of Christ and asks him to bless and sanctify the water to the souls of all who partake of it.

"In remembrance of the blood of thy Son, which was shed for them." The blood of Christ is often referred to as the cleansing agent through which our sins are washed away. Jesus taught, "And no unclean thing can enter into his kingdom; therefore nothing entereth into his rest save it be those who have washed their garments in my blood, because of their faith, and the repentance of all their sins, and their faithfulness unto the end" (3 Nephi 27:19).

I used to think that the next five words in the prayer, "which was shed for them," were simply a reminder that Jesus performed the Atonement for us and shed his blood in the process. But the Bible Dictionary explains, "The atoning power of a sacrifice was in the blood because it was regarded as containing the life of the animal and because the sacrifice was a type of the great sacrifice who is Jesus Christ (Leviticus 17:11; Hebrews 9:22). The scripture says that 'almost all things are by the law purged with blood; and without shedding of blood is no remission' (Hebrews 9:22). Jesus worked out a perfect atonement by the shedding of his own blood" (Bible Dictionary, 626).

Those five extra words, "which was shed for them," are vital, because without the shedding of blood there is no remission! Like the ancient sacrifices that shed blood as a type of things to come, the blood of Jesus was was shed for the remission of our sins.

"That they may witness unto thee, O God, the Eternal Father, that they do always remember him." In the prayer over the bread, we "witness" that we are willing to take upon us the name of Christ, always remember him, and keep his commandments. In the prayer over the water, the wording is different: we do not covenant that we are *willing* to always remember him but that we *do* always remember him. It sounds to me like we must remember right now, in the present, and perhaps even in the recent past, and not just commit to some future effort.

In both prayers, we covenant to remember. President Marion G. Romney remarked, "It is said of President Wilford Woodruff that while the sacrament was being passed, his lips could be observed in silent motion as he repeated to himself over and over again, "I do remember thee, I do remember thee" ("Reverence," *Ensign,* October 1976, 3).

WHY ARE THERE TWO PRAYERS?

One prayer is for the bread, the other for the water. Because of Jesus' body, represented by the bread, every single person will be resurrected and live forever. That's immortality. Because of Jesus' blood, represented by the water, those who repent and keep their covenants can again live with the Father and the Son. That's eternal life.

Immortality and eternal life are not the same thing. Immortality means you won't ever die. Everyone will have that because everyone will be resurrected. Eternal life is the kind of life God lives, which is made possible by the Atonement.

With that in mind, read Moses 1:39: "For behold, this is my work and my glory—to bring to pass the immortality [the bread] and eternal life [the water] of man."

I suppose the best answer to the question of why the Lord gave two sacrament prayers is that he designed the ordinance that way. But we can also see that there is a difference between what was accomplished by Jesus' body and by Jesus' blood.

Till We Meet Again

In order to be a covenant people, we must make a covenant. We, as Latter-day Saints, are blessed with the opportunity to renew baptismal covenants on a weekly basis. As I said before, I wish someone would've explained all this to me when I was a deacon! Maybe someone tried, and I just wasn't listening.

Now, in my Melchizedek Priesthood years, I know exactly where I'll be each Sunday. I know I'll have some time to sit and think. I know I'll have the opportunity to review the week, as well as my life. I'll always be grateful for the opportunity to meet with people of faith, renew soul-restoring covenants, and review in my mind the words of what just might be Heavenly Father's favorite scripture.

6

<u>Fast Offerings</u>

I thought it was a great honor to be a deacon. My father was always considerate of my responsibilities and always permitted me to take the buggy and horse to gather fast offerings. My responsibility included that part of the town in which I lived, but it was quite a long walk to the homes, and a sack of flour or a bottle of fruit or vegetables or bread became quite heavy as it accumulated. So the buggy was very comfortable and functional. We have changed to cash in later days, but it was commodities in my day. It was a very great honor to do this service for my Heavenly Father: and though times have changed, when money is given generally instead of commodities, it is still a great honor to perform this service (Spencer W. Kimball, The Teachings of Spencer W. Kimball, *ed. Edward L. Kimball [Salt Lake City: Bookcraft, 1982], 146).*

"Fast Sunday is the slowest day of the month." That's what I remember about fast Sundays as a boy. I didn't realize then that fast Sunday is all about helping people. Yes, you skip your evening snack and your morning bowl of Cap'n Crunch, but you go hungry so that others can eat! Fasting also benefits you by helping you develop self-control. Elder Russell M. Nelson said, "Fasting gives you confidence to know that your spirit can master appetite" ("Self-Mastery," *Ensign,* November 1985, 30–31).

Your "fast offering" is the money that your family donates to the ward that you normally would spend on food. Some people donate much more than the cost of two meals to help those in need.

If all you think about is your stomach, you're not really fasting—you're just going hungry. In that case, fast Sunday really does pass slowly, and your fasting becomes little more than an inexpensive diet.

President Gordon B. Hinckley teaches us not to focus on the hunger part of fasting. He thinks fasting is so wonderful that everyone should try it! He said:

> It is not a burden to refrain from two meals a month and give the value thereof to assist in caring for the poor. It is, rather, a blessing. Not only will physical benefits flow from the observance of this principle, but spiritual values also. Our program of the fast day and the fast offering is so simple and so beautiful that I cannot understand why people everywhere do not take it up (*Teachings of Gordon B. Hinckley* [Salt Lake City: Deseret Book, 1997], 217–18).

What does this have to do with the Aaronic Priesthood? Well, try to get your mind off Cap'n Crunch, and I'll tell you. One of the duties of a deacon is to collect fast offerings. But don't lose your perspective! You're doing more than just walking door to door.

 You've probably heard the story about the three bricklayers. Each of them was doing the same difficult work, but each had a different outlook. When asked what they were doing, the first one replied, "I'm laying bricks." The second one, with a broader vision, said, "I'm building a wall." The third bricklayer had the best perspective of all. He looked up and answered with pride, "I'm building a cathedral."

So as a deacon, you're not just walking from house to house and ringing doorbells. And you're not just "collecting fast offerings" either. You're doing the Lord's work by helping the poor. As you read the scriptures, you will discover that Jesus was always concerned about the poor.

Now, go out and ask anybody in the world, "How many twelve- and thirteen-year-olds do you know who dress up in a shirt and tie once a month and go out to help the poor?" Most people won't know any.

But you and I know dozens. They're called *deacons.* Deacons are incredible. Are you beginning to see how amazing it is to hold the priesthood?

The next time it's fast Sunday and you're thinking about your empty stomach, let it remind you of how many other empty stomachs there are in the world, and how each month you can do something to help the empty stomachs in your own neighborhood.

I pray that we may so sense the value of the priesthood, that every deacon in this Church will realize that when he is given the Aaronic Priesthood he is set apart among his fellows, that he is different from others. He cannot with impunity swear as other boys may swear; he cannot participate in pranks in the neighborhood as other boys may participate; he stands apart. That is what it means to a twelve-year-old boy, and, bishops, that is just what you should explain to them when you choose them to be deacons. Do not just call them up and ordain them, but have a talk with them and let them realize what it means to be given the Aaronic Priesthood. In the boyhood area these boys so chosen and instructed should exert an influence for good (David O. McKay, Con-ference Report, *October 1948, 174).*

7

Honor

We've talked about some wonderful things so far, and I'm glad you're still with me. The title of this book is *Honoring the Priesthood*. What exactly do we mean by that?

In Exodus 20:12, we read that the fifth commandment is to "honour thy father and thy mother." A footnote to that scripture says that to honor means to "respect, or value." My dictionary tells me that to honor means to "hold in high respect; to revere." (Notice that the word *revere* is the first part of the word *reverence*.) When I think of honoring the priesthood, I think of those two "R" words: respect and reverence.

The words *respect* and *reverence* aren't very popular in the world today. There are no television sitcoms about respect and reverence. You'll never see a new hit movie titled *Respect and Reverence,* or a website called "respectandreverence.com." Sports heroes and rock stars are not honored for their respect and reverence but more often for their recklessness and rowdiness. Sadly, many who are portrayed as heroes are arrogant and crude.

This is just one of the things I love about our church. It expects extraordinary things from us. It teaches us that we cannot be average or ordinary or go with the crowd. I've never heard a talk called "Be Average" or "Just Act Like Everybody Else." I've never heard counsel in general conference to become lazy or worldly or common. We don't have Sunday School lessons that teach us to become slackers and whiners.

Instead, we are invited to be exceptional, extraordinary, and valiant. We hear talks and lessons about honor and courage and responsibility and respect. Our leaders want us to be awarded in a court of honor, not arraigned in a court of law. We're encouraged to be different, or "peculiar," but in a positive way. The Apostle Peter wrote, "Ye are a chosen generation, a royal priesthood, an holy nation, a peculiar people; that ye should shew forth the praises of him who hath called you out of darkness into his marvellous light" (1 Peter 2:9).

I guess these talks and lessons are working. After all, look at yourself! You must be pretty impressive because you're reading a book about honor and respect and reverence. How many teenage boys are doing what you're doing right now? Very few, I'll bet. The Lord, his Church, and your priesthood leaders expect great things of you, and the wonderful thing is, you're living up to those expectations.

We've talked about what the priesthood is, and what our duties are, but the priesthood is not just an office with a list of duties. It is a full-time responsibility that we should always honor.

Bishop H. David Burton, the Church's presiding bishop, said, "The priesthood isn't something we take off during the week and put on for Sunday. It is a 24–7 privilege and blessing—that is, 24 hours a day, 7 days a week" ("Honoring the Priesthood," *Ensign,* May 2000, 39).

Every word you speak, every person you talk to, every movie you watch, every conversation you participate in, every date you go on, your priesthood is there with you.

In these next few chapters, we'll talk about honoring the priesthood in the way you dress, the way you talk, the way you interact with young women, and the way you choose to be entertained.

DID YOU KNOW?

In 1830–31, Titus Billings, Serenus Burnett, and John Burk became the first deacons ordained in the restored Church (William G. Hartley, "Deacon Power," in *Priesthood in Action* [Salt Lake City: New Era, 1986], 67).

The word deacon comes from the Greek work *diakonos,* meaning "servant" *(Encyclopedia of Mormonism,* ed. Daniel H. Ludlow, 4 vols. [New York: Macmillan, 1992], 1:361).

WILFORD WOODRUFF:

"All the organizations of the priesthood have power. The Deacon has power, through the priesthood which he holds. So has the Teacher. They have power to go before the Lord and have their prayers heard and answered, as well as the prophet, the seer, or the revelator has. It is by this priesthood that the work of God has been accomplished. It is by this priesthood that men have ordinances conferred upon them, that their sins are forgiven, and that they are redeemed. For this purpose has it been revealed and sealed upon our heads" (*The Discourses of Wilford Woodruff,* ed. G. Homer Durham [Salt Lake City: Bookcraft, 1969], 69).

8

Dress with Dignity and Class

A great tug-of-war is going on. Both sides are pulling, and you're in the middle. But you have the strength to choose the winner. Neither side can successfully pull you to one side or the other without your consent.

One side, the Lord's side, reminds you of your baptismal covenants—"to stand as a witness of God at all times and in all things, and in all places" (Mosiah 18:9). The other side, the world's side, wants you to forget your covenants. You were created in the image of God, but the pull of the world wants you to be in the image of the world. The image of the world these days is body piercing, tattoos, earrings, sloppy or extreme hairstyles, and shabby and immodest clothing. The voice of the

Lord, through his servants, has given us guidelines to follow in the *For the Strength of Youth* booklet:

The way you dress is a reflection of what you are on the inside. . . . When you are well groomed and modestly dressed, you invite the companionship of the Spirit and can exercise a good influence on those around you. . . . All should avoid extremes in clothing, appearance, and hairstyle. Always be neat and clean and avoid being sloppy or inappropriately casual in dress, grooming, and manners. . . . Do not disfigure yourself with tattoos or body piercings (*For the Strength of Youth: Fulfilling Our Duty to God* [Salt Lake City: The Church of Jesus Christ of Latter-day Saints, 2001], 14–16).

Someone might respond, "It's my body. I can do what I want with it." Hmmm, is it really? Maybe some of the Saints in ancient Corinth felt the same way. This is what Paul wrote to them: "What? Know ye not that your body is the temple of the Holy Ghost which is in you, which ye have of God, and ye are not your own? For ye are bought with a price: therefore glorify God in your body, and in your spirit, which are God's" (1 Corinthians 6:19–20).

If we think that disfiguring our bodies is no big deal, we'd better think again. President Spencer W. Kimball once made a fascinating statement about our resurrected bodies.

> This body will come forth in the resurrection. It will be free from all imperfections and scars and infirmities which came to it in mortality which were not self-inflicted. Would we have a right to expect a perfect body if we carelessly or intentionally damaged it?
>
> We shall have our resurrected, perfected bodies through the eternities. They were given to us—we had little to do with getting them.
>
> It then becomes our duty to protect them from hazards, from mutilation or disfigurement. We should treat them well, building them with proper foods, proper rest, proper exercise and keep them strong, robust, beautiful, and undamaged and live on and on till called home by our Lord (*The Teachings of Spencer W. Kimball,* ed. Edward L. Kimball [Salt Lake City: Bookcraft, 1982], 36).

What happens to those who ignore the voice of the Lord and his servants, and allow the image of the world to pull them in?

The day cometh that they who will not hear the voice of the Lord, neither the voice of his servants, neither give heed to the words of the prophets and apostles, shall be cut off from among the people. . . . They seek not the Lord to establish his righteousness, but every man walketh in his own way, and after the image of his own god, whose image is in the likeness of the world (D&C 1:14, 16).

Some young people are trying very hard to look just like the world. Perhaps they don't realize that they're following a false god—the god of popular opinion, or, in other words, the god of the "likeness of the world." The priesthood calls us to rise above the world and to be a light to the world. If we don't heed that call, we become just another chunk of driftwood, caught in the currents of fashion and "going with the flow" to the gulf of misery. What good is having a living prophet if we don't listen to him?

The classiest, most dignified dress, for men of any age, is a white shirt and tie. This is why Aaronic Priesthood age young men are specifically counseled to wear a white shirt when they administer the sacrament. Elder Jeffrey R. Holland explained:

May I suggest that wherever possible a white shirt be worn by the deacons, teachers, and priests who handle the sacrament. For sacred ordinances in the Church we often use ceremonial clothing, and a white shirt could be seen as a gentle reminder of the white clothing you wore in the baptismal font and in anticipation of the white shirt you will soon wear into the temple and onto your missions ("'This Do in Remembrance of Me,'" *Ensign,* November 1995, 68).

When you face your closet at the beginning of each day, remember that what you wear is another opportunity to honor your priesthood. People will make assumptions about your beliefs based on what you wear, so dress with honor.

When you face your closet on Sunday morning, ask yourself, "What does the Lord deserve? What would Jesus, who suffered, bled, and died for me, want me to wear today?" If you ask yourself these questions, the answer will be obvious. *The Lord gave me his best, so he deserves the best from me—my Sunday best.*

Yes, there's a big tug-of-war going on, and you're in the middle. You decide who wins. You decide which God you will serve—the eternal, living God

of heaven or the lifeless, changing god of popular opinion. I think I know which side you're on. If you've read this far, I have little doubt. I can almost hear you say, "Choose you this day whom ye will serve; . . . but as for me and my house, we will serve the Lord" (Joshua 24:15).

When thinking about standards regarding dress or movies or music, it may help to imagine a large tree with a sturdy trunk, numerous strong branches, and hundreds of leaves. Now think of the trunk as *doctrines,* the branches as *principles,* and the leaves as *rules. Rules* come from *principles,* which come from *doctrines.* Deacons, teachers, and priests wear white shirts because that's the rule. But rules aren't just made up. The rule to wear a white shirt comes from the *principle* of reverence and respect for sacred things. The sacrament is sacred and connected to the *doctrine* of the Atonement, and no doctrine is more important than the atonement of Jesus Christ.

I'm convinced that if the young men of the Aaronic Priesthood understood the doctrine of the Atonement and the principle of reverence, they would have no problem with the rule.

In the next chapter, you'll read about rules for choosing entertainment, such as movies, television, music, internet sites, and computer games. See if you can find the principles and doctrines involved as you read.

9

Modern Media

You will find that one of the greatest challenges of honoring your priesthood is in keeping your thoughts clean. It takes constant effort because of the things we see and hear all around us. Therefore, we must take control of the input. Computers can't think for themselves. They do what their software tells them to do. That's why computer pro-grammers and technical support people often quote this little poem:

> My computer is a crazy thing
> I wish that I could sell it.
> It never does the things I want
> But only what I tell it.
> (Author unknown)

Computers respond to their input. If their input is bad, their output will be bad. Another phrase common to those who use computers is "GIGO," or "Garbage in, garbage out." We can't give a computer bad data and expect good results. But if our computers have corrupted input, we can delete files and reformat hard drives, which will leave no trace of bad data.

Our brains are different. They are much more complex than even today's supercomputers, but some of the same rules apply. Where do our brains get input? From what we *see* and what we *hear*. But with our brains, it's not GIGO, it's GIGS: "Garbage in, garbage *stays*." Our brains can't delete input. That's why we have to carefully control what we see and what we listen to. Elder Dallin H. Oaks said:

> The body has defenses to rid itself of unwholesome food, but the brain won't vomit back filth. Once recorded it will always remain subject to recall, flashing its perverted images across your mind, and drawing you away from the wholesome things in life (cited by N. Eldon Tanner in "No Greater Honor: The Woman's Role," *Ensign*, January 1974, 8).

Another result of filling our minds with the bad is that the good is forced into the background. When this happens, we feel less worthy and our faith and confidence in Christ decrease. Elder H. Burke Peterson said:

> When we see or hear anything filthy or vulgar, whatever the source, our mind records it, and as it makes the filthy record, beauty and clean thoughts are pushed into the background. Hope and faith in Christ begin to fade, and more and more, turmoil and discontent become our companions (" 'Touch Not the Evil Gift, nor the Unclean Thing,' " *Ensign,* November 1993, 43).

Faith in the Lord Jesus Christ is the first principle of the gospel (A of F 1:4), so naturally Satan makes it his first principle to pollute our minds with things that make our thoughts unworthy and that erode our faith in Christ.

SATAN'S SMART WEAPONS

We are living in a day of amazing technology. We have tools that have made worldwide communication almost instantaneous. But any powerful and useful tool can also be used as a destructive weapon.

Satan uses today's computer technology to target young people and deliver his weapons right into their home. It used to be that if you wanted pornography, you had to go to a store and buy it. You'd have to look a cashier in the eye. You'd probably be ashamed of yourself and hope you weren't recognized. But technology has made it easier to get the bad stuff anonymously—first through VCRs, then from cable TV, and later by satellite. Great things have come from these technological developments, but at the same time they have allowed people to bring some of the worst of what the world has to offer right into their living rooms.

Then the technology improved again. Now, you don't have to leave home to find evil. It finds you. If you have unfiltered internet access in your home, Satan can plant a smart bomb right on your desk. Elder Richard G. Scott warned:

> One of the most damning influences on earth, one that has caused uncountable grief, suffering, heartache, and destroyed marriages is the onslaught of pornography in all of its vicious, corroding, destructive forms. Whether it be through the printed page, movies, television, obscene lyrics, the telephone, or on a flickering personal computer

screen, pornography is overpoweringly addictive and severely damaging ("Making the Right Choices," *Ensign*, November 1994, 37).

"OVERPOWERINGLY ADDICTIVE"

Think about a fishing lure. When pulled through the water, it is flashy and attractive to fish. The fish think it's something good, but it's fake! They're attracted to it, but they only see the flash and color—they don't see the danger. Look closely at a fishhook. Notice that it has two sharp ends, not one. The outside point hooks the fish first. Then, when the fish tries to let go, it's hooked by the second point, called a barb. Once the fish is hooked, the fisherman takes control of the fish's life.

Young men, let's be blunt. Pornography is frightening stuff. It hooks people, and as hard as they struggle, many find that they can't let go. It destroys their lives. It fills them with guilt and remorse. It robs them of happiness. So I offer this advice with great intensity: Don't look at it, don't toy with it, and don't even get near it—not even once. This is one of Satan's deadliest, scariest weapons, and it has a barb. Satan sees many big fish out there, particularly the priesthood holders of the Church. Because technology has made pornography easier to find than it used to be, Satan is catching a few who wouldn't have been caught twenty years ago. Perhaps this is why Elder Scott said:

> Satan particularly seeks to tempt one who has lived a pure, clean life to experiment through magazines, videocassettes, or movies with powerful images of a woman's body. He wants to stimulate appetite to cause experimentation that quickly results in intimacies and defilement. Powerful habits are formed which are difficult to break. Mental and emotional scars result ("Making the Right Choices," 38).

If you have a problem with pornography, there is hope. Sometimes big fish get away. The help you need comes from the priesthood. If pornography is a problem for you, please go see your bishop as soon as possible. My friend Brad Wilcox has written:

> In private interviews, some bishops ask directly about pornography while others do not. Either way, if pornography is a problem for you, you need to seek help. Those who have courage to admit

their struggle to a bishop or parent usually find a valuable friend and ally.

A commitment made to yourself can easily be broken. Commitments to God are often easily postponed. But commitments made to another person put pressure on us. . . . If you struggle with pornography and know you will be seeing a bishop on Sunday morning, you may think twice about what you do on Saturday night.

However, as helpful as a spoken commitment to your bishop can be, that is far from being the only reason to see your bishop. As the father for the ward, he is authorized to receive revelation on your behalf. He can give you priesthood blessings and inspired counsel. He can help you formulate a positive plan of action and use priesthood keys to assist you in your quest to repent, draw closer to the Savior, and claim the wonderful blessings of Jesus Christ's atonement. Your parents can play a similar positive role if you feel comfortable asking them for help. You will be amazed at the changes you can make when you stop relying on willpower alone and start relying on God's power (*Growing Up: Gospel Answers About Maturation and Sex* [Salt Lake City: Bookcraft, 2000], 117–18).

When I was a boy in the Aaronic Priesthood, most of the standards talks I heard were about smoking and drinking and the Word of Wisdom. We didn't hear as many talks about sexual immorality. I believe that things have changed, and I believe that because of advances in technology, Satan's tactics have changed. Of course, the Word of Wisdom is just as important as it was before, but Satan is now armed with stealthy, smart, brutal, covert weapons, and he's after us. President Ezra Taft Benson taught:

> The plaguing sin of this generation is sexual immorality. This, the Prophet Joseph said, would be the source of more temptations, more buffetings, and more difficulties for the elders of Israel than any other (*The Teachings of Ezra Taft Benson* [Salt Lake City: Bookcraft, 1988], 277).

If we never look at pornography, we won't be in danger of becoming addicted. In the last days, much of the self-control we'll have to exercise will be what we choose to look at. The Savior taught, "And verily I say unto you, as I have said before, he that looketh on a woman to lust after her, or if any shall commit adultery in their hearts, they shall not have the Spirit, but shall deny the faith and shall fear" (D&C 63:16; 42:23).

MAYBE JUST A LITTLE BIT WON'T HURT, RIGHT?

Oh, sure. Imagine of bunch of trout having a meeting at the bottom of a lake. Do you think any of them would say, "Well, it isn't that fishhooks are bad, just bite them in moderation; a little bite doesn't hurt"? No way. All it takes is one lure and you're hooked (then cooked). *For the Strength of Youth* warns:

> Pornography in all its forms is especially danger-ous and addictive. What may begin as a curious indulgence can become a destructive habit that takes control of your life. It can lead you to sexual trans-gression and even criminal behavior. Pornography is a poison that weakens your self-control, changes the way you see others, causes you to lose the guidance of the Spirit, and can even affect your ability to have a normal relationship with your future spouse. If you encounter pornography, turn away from it immediately (*For the Strength of Youth: Fulfilling Our Duty to God* [Salt Lake City: The Church of Jesus Christ of Latter-day Saints, 2001], 17–19).

The message is clear—a little bit *can* hurt! A little bit can hook! You may have noticed that some of the very last words in the Book of Mormon are these:

> And again I would exhort you that ye would come unto Christ, and lay hold upon every good gift, and touch not the evil gift, nor the unclean thing. . . . Yea, come unto Christ, and be perfected in him, and deny yourselves of all ungodliness (Moroni 10:30, 32).

Notice that Moroni doesn't say, "Just a little is okay," or "Partake of evil in moderation." He says *don't even touch it,* and "deny yourselves of all ungodliness." It's too bad we have to spend time in this book talking about the bad stuff, because there's so much good out there! And as holders of the priesthood, we're to come unto Christ and lay hold on all the good, wonderful, honorable things the world has to offer.

TELEVISION AND MOVIES

Modern media include not only the internet but also television and movies. We talked about the internet first because it's probably the most dangerous right now. Now let's change channels and talk about television and movies.

When I was born, the shows on television included, *I Love Lucy, The Dick Van Dyke Show, Leave it to Beaver,* and, my personal favorite, *The Andy Griffith Show.* Although these programs are nearly forty years old, you may have seen some of them because the reruns are still popular. If I wanted to watch TV all day when I was a kid, my parents would have been concerned only because I was wasting my time. Today, most of the stuff on TV can be spiritually lethal. Elder Jeffrey R. Holland spoke on this topic to the men and boys of the priesthood:

> With modern technology even your youngest brothers and sisters can be carried virtually around the world before they are old enough to ride a tricycle safely across the street. What were in my generation carefree moments of moviegoing, TV watching, and magazine reading have now, with the additional availability of VCRs, the Internet, and personal computers, become *amusements* fraught with genuine moral danger. I put the word *amusements* in italics. Did you know that the original Latin meaning of the word *amusement* is "a

diversion of the mind intended to deceive"? Unfortunately that is largely what "amusements" in our day have again become in the hands of the arch deceiver (" 'Sanctify Yourselves,' " *Ensign,* November 2000, 39).

The television networks used to censor themselves and limit crude words and immoral situations. You could watch every episode of the TV shows I mentioned above and never hear one curse word or one vulgar joke. Things have changed dramatically. Now the networks seem to be trying to get the very worst things they can onto the screen. Watch a primetime TV show today, and you'll hear profanity and vulgarity in the first scene. It seems that with each new year, the network censors allow a new curse word or a new immoral situation to be broadcast through the airwaves. They are sinking to new lows, which is why we can no longer assume that anything on TV is safe.

 Also, many cable channels now show the type of full-length movies that those under seventeen could not attend at a theater. All of this means that we're going to have to guard the door to our home theater and replace the remote

control with self-control. *For the Strength of Youth* gives us a clear guideline:

> Do not attend, view, or participate in entertainment that is vulgar, immoral, violent, or pornographic in any way. Do not participate in entertainment that in any way presents immorality or violent behavior as acceptable (*For the Strength of Youth,* 17).

If the programs we watch do not meet the standard described above, then they offend the Spirit and we lose the benefit of the gift of the Holy Ghost. Without the Holy Ghost, we lose important guidance and protection, and we make worse decisions, which can lead to even more trouble.

MUSIC

Have you ever been sitting in a car at an intersection when you notice your car beginning to vibrate to a drumbeat coming from another car way behind you? Some people love their music so much that they want everyone to hear it. The latest car stereo systems have amplifiers and speakers so large that they can be heard in multiple area codes.

I love music. I play the trumpet, drums, guitar, banjo, a little piano, and I'm really good at the CD player. But music, like everything else, can be an influence for good or bad. Satan is determined to

take away your guide and protector, the gift of the Holy Ghost. If you read the entire *For the Strength of Youth* booklet, you will notice that the standard for all modern

media comes down to one principle: Don't partake of things that offend the Spirit. Music is no exception: "Don't listen to music that *drives away the Spirit,* encourages immorality, glorifies violence, uses foul or offensive language, or promotes Satanism or other evil practices" (*For the Strength of Youth,* 20; emphasis added).

Deep down, you know what you should do with music that offends the Spirit. Because you *know what to do,* you must *do what you know.* That's what being a man is all about. So the music standard is as simple as the other standards. If it offends the Lord, it should offend you too.

In his last talk as a general authority, Elder H. Burke Peterson said:

Brethren, I plead with you to leave it alone. Stay away from any movie, video, publication, or music—*regardless of its rating*—where illicit behavior and expressions are a part of the action. Have the courage to turn it off in your living room. Throw the tapes and the publications in the garbage can, for that is where we keep garbage. . . .

Again I say, leave it alone. Turn it off, walk away from it, burn it, erase it, destroy it. I know it is hard counsel we give when we say movies that are R-rated, and many with PG-13 ratings, are produced by satanic influences. Our standards should not be dictated by the rating system. I repeat, because of what they *really* represent, these types of movies, music, tapes, etc. serve the purposes of the author of all darkness (" 'Touch Not the Evil Gift, nor the Unclean Thing,' " *Ensign,* November 1993, 43).

We have been warned again and again, now we have to act. As priesthood holders, you and I must be "doers of the word, and not hearers only" (James 1:22).

SUMMARY

We have responsibility for controlling the "input" into our mental computers. We can't give that responsibility to an uninspired ratings board or to an internet service provider. To honor our priesthood means to take charge of what we choose to see and hear. The Lord has given us counsel in deciding what we watch, and we must rise up, be men, and take a stand! Of course, recent inventions can give us some help too. We have internet filters, V-chips, and TV ratings, and we're happy to use these tools. But we have something even better. The *best* internet filter, the *most effective* V-chip, and the *most accurate* rating system will always be the Holy Ghost. If a TV program, video game, internet site, CD, book, or movie offends the Holy Ghost, it will also offend any righteous priesthood holder who is worthy of the gift of the Holy Ghost.

In the standards we just reviewed, did you watch for the trunk, branches, and leaves that we mentioned at the end of the last chapter? What did you notice? It seems to me that the rules concerning movies, music, and other media all grow from the principle of keeping the Spirit with you. And the importance of keeping the Spirit with you comes from one sturdy trunk—the doctrine of the gift of the Holy Ghost! Satan wants to take away that priceless gift so that you'll lose your guide and protection and make poor decisions. Living gospel standards, or the "rules," will ensure that you keep that gift and that you become what your Father in Heaven wants you to become.

TEN REASONS WHY I SWEAR

1. It pleases my mother so much.
2. It is a fine mark of manliness.
3. It proves I have self-control.
4. It indicates how clearly my mind operates.
5. It makes my conversation so pleasing to everyone.
6. It leaves no doubt in anyone's mind as to my good breeding.
7. It impresses people that I have more than an ordinary education.
8. It is an unmistakable sign of culture and refinement.
9. It makes me a very desirable personality among women and children of culture and refinement.
10. It is my way of honoring God, who said, "Thou shalt not take the name of the Lord in vain" (from a tract by Alex Dunlap).

10

If You Had to Eat Your Words, Would They Make You Sick?

When my friend Dave Hyde was in high school, he had a chance to earn some extra credit in his biology class. All he had to do was eat some deer meat to earn five points. Dave ate it. Rattlesnake meat was worth seven points. Dave gulped it. Then the teacher pulled out some caviar (fish eggs). All Dave had to do was swallow a spoonful for another ten points. Dave swallowed it. These tasty delights were followed by some worm cookies and cow brain casserole, but the big bonus was yet to come. Worth twenty-five points, it consisted of a jar of dead ants.

"All the students started to squirm and make disgusting sounds when the teacher brought out the jar," Dave recalled. "I was the only one to go to the front, and the teacher said, 'Okay Hyde, tilt your head back and open your mouth wide.' He then took a heaping spoonful of dead ants and poured them into my mouth. He then physically closed my mouth, and I began to munch and crunch. Halfway through my chewing, the class began to make me laugh. My lips separated and I think the class could see all these ant legs and body parts all over my teeth. I remember the taste as being pretty bitter. My grade moved up pretty dramatically that day. I only wish my social life with the ladies had. For some strange reason, it didn't. My biology class was just before lunch, and someone asked if I had already had my lunch because it looked like I had a piece of pepper caught in my teeth. 'No, it's probably just an ant head.'"

Dave ate all that stuff on Tuesday, May 13. They pumped his stomach on Wednesday, May 14 (just kidding). Yuck. I think I'd rather get a bad grade than eat leftovers from the biology lab. Now here's another thought: What if your science teacher said you had to eat your words? Are the words that come out of your mouth in bad taste? Are there things you say that are foul and gross? If you had to eat your words, would they make you sick? If so, then maybe the old saying—"You are what you eat"—is true.

YOU DON'T SAY . . .

This book is about honoring your priesthood. The Lord expects you, as an Aaronic Priesthood holder, to control your tongue. You can't hold the power of God and be a potty mouth at the same time. President Gordon B. Hinckley said:

> Most of you boys who are here tonight are prospective missionaries. It is as wrong for you to use foul language as it would be for a missionary because you also hold the priesthood. You have authority to act in the name of God. Remember that it is the same voice which prays to the Lord on the one hand and which, on the other hand, when in the company of friends, may be inclined so to speak language foul and filthy. The two kinds of voices are incompatible ("Take Not the Name of God in Vain," *Ensign,* November 1987, 47).

Some of you are, or one day will be, priests. President Hinckley reminds you that you have the same mouth Monday through Friday that you have on Saturday and Sunday. How can you pronounce the prayer on the sacrament one day and swear at school the next day? James said it like this: "Out of the same mouth proceedeth blessing and cursing. My brethren, these things ought not so to be" (James 3:10).

Profanity is not macho, manly, or mature. It's low-class, low-level language and, like it or not, people will judge you by the words you speak. When they judge you, they judge the Church and the priesthood as well. Wouldn't it be sad if a few of us gave a horrible impression about the rest of us? And what about the impression you make about yourself? They say that "sticks and stones may break my bones but words will never hurt me." That's true when you're learning to respond to bad things said about you. But your *own* words, coming out of your own mouth, have great potential to hurt you—they tell the whole world all about you. Harmful words not only include swear words but also substitute swear words, or words that are vulgar and show very little class. So make sure the words that come out of your mouth represent the best of what you are within.

Put in a Good Word for Yourself

Bad language can give you a bad reputation, but it works the other way too. Good language and good conversation can help you develop a good reputation. I've met young people who simply refuse to curse and swear. After a while, their friends notice, and their friends stop swearing too. Or, when others start to swear, their friends say, "Hey, don't talk that way around him." President Gordon B. Hinckley said:

> Cultivate the art of conversation. It is a tremendous asset. For me there is nothing more delightful than to listen in on the conversation of a group of bright and happy young people such as you. Their dialogue is witty. It is scintillating. It sparkles and is punctuated by laughing even when dealing with serious subjects. But, I repeat, it is not necessary in conversation to profane the name of Deity or to use salty and salacious language of any kind. And let me add that there is plenty of humor in the world without resorting to what we speak of as dirty jokes ("True to the Faith," *Ensign,* June 1996, 6).

We admire professional athletes. They can run and catch and shoot and pivot and dribble and make it all look easy. They have remarkable control of their bodies. It's too bad, however, that more athletes, and more people in general, don't have better control of their tongues. Controlling your tongue is so difficult that the scriptures speak of those with tongue control as "perfect." James said, "If any man offend not in word, the same is a perfect man, and able also to bridle the whole body" (James 3:2).

In other words, if you discipline yourself to control your tongue, you can also "bridle," or control, your whole body. As a priesthood holder myself, I would like to share with you two scriptures and two quotations that really help me control my words.

Here's the first scripture: "But I say unto you, that every idle word that men shall speak, they shall give account thereof in the day of judgment" (Matthew 12:36). I can't even remember all the stupid things I've said over the years, but it appears they'll all come out in the judgment unless I repent.

Here's the second one (and this is probably the scariest scripture I've ever read): "For our words will condemn us, yea, all our works will condemn us; we shall not be found spotless; and our thoughts will also condemn us; and in this awful state we shall not dare to look up to our God; and we would fain be glad if we could command the rocks and the mountains to fall upon us to hide us from his presence" (Alma 12:14).

Controlling the tongue isn't just about swearing or cursing. It's also about backbiting and gossiping. Cutting people down behind their back dishonors the priesthood, and it shows a lack of control. You've seen the two scriptures, now here are the two quotations I mentioned that have really helped me.

> Boys flying kites haul in their white-winged birds;
> You can call back your kites, but you can't call back
>   your words.
> "Careful with fire" is good advice, we know;
> "Careful with words" is ten times doubly so.
> Thoughts unexpressed will often fall back dead.
> But God Himself can't kill them, once they are said!
>
>> (Will Carleton, "The First Settler's Story," cited in Boyd K. Packer, "Balm of Gilead," *Ensign,* November 1987, 16–17)

This poem reminds me that even if I apologize for something I said, the memory of it will remain in the minds of those who heard me say it. So it's better to control your tongue in the first place. Here's the second quotation I really like (someday I'm going to have it framed and placed above my family's dinner table):

> Great minds talk about ideas.
> Average minds talk about things.
> Small minds talk about people.
>
> (Anonymous)

The people I respect and admire most rarely talk about other people. If they do, it's always in a respectful, careful way. Instead, they prefer to talk about ideas, usually gospel ideas. That's the kind of dinner conversation that's enlightening, sometimes even testimony building. It's so much different than chewing someone up between mouthfuls.

The next time you're around the people you respect and admire most, watch them closely, and make mental notes of what they talk about. If they had to eat their words, would their meal be hard to swallow like high school floor sweepings? Or would it be sweet and delicious like a gourmet meal?

WHAT THE LORD EXPECTS

DOCTRINE AND COVENANTS 20:60:

"Every elder, priest, teacher, or deacon is to be ordained according to the gifts and callings of God unto him; and he is to be ordained by the power of the Holy Ghost, which is in the one who ordains him."

DOCTRINE AND COVENANTS 20:53–55:

"The teacher's duty is to watch over the church always, and be with and strengthen them; and see that there is no iniquity in the church, neither hardness with each other, neither lying, backbiting, nor evil speaking; and see that the church meet together often, and also see that all the members do their duty."

DOCTRINE AND COVENANTS 20:46–48:

"The priest's duty is to preach, teach, expound, exhort, and baptize, and administer the sacrament, and visit the house of each member, and exhort them to pray vocally and in secret and attend to all family duties. And he may also ordain other priests, teachers, and deacons."

11

Honor Your Priesthood by Respecting Young Women

As you grow from deacon to teacher to priest, one of your favorite topics will become young women. (If your favorite topic is still PlayStation, well, read this chapter anyway.) We are all in this church together, and the young men and young women can support and help each other as they strive to live the gospel and build the kingdom.

As an Aaronic Priesthood holder, you can have a powerful impact on the young women you know. In fact, some of them may need your example and help. They need to know that because you honor your priesthood, you value virtue and modesty. You might even have to open your mouth and tell them so! Elder Richard G. Scott, speaking at general priesthood meeting, said:

So many of our own young women sacrifice their God-given endowment of femininity, deep spirituality, and a caring interest in others on the altar of popular, worldly opinion. Young men, let such young women know that you will not seek an eternal companion from those that are overcome by worldly trends. Many dress and act immodestly because they are told that is what you want. In sensitive ways, communicate how distasteful revealing attire is to you, a worthy young man, and how it stimulates unwanted emotions from what you see against your will ("The Sanctity of Womanhood," *Ensign,* May 2000, 36–37).

Let the young women in your ward know that the girls who dress immodestly may get attention, but it's based on how they look on the outside, not on who they are on the inside. Let the young women know that popularity is different from respect. Some girls who dress or act immodestly might be popular with some guys, but they might not be respected. Let the young women know that you are more attracted to a fun, outgoing personality than to a worldly look. I believe they will listen very closely to what you say. You may not know it, and you may not believe it, but there are probably a few Beehives, Mia Maids, and Laurels watching what you do every week. I'll bet they would be very interested in your opinion. Make sure they can look up to you as an honorable priesthood holder.

IF THE YOUNG WOMEN COULD TALK TO YOU, WHAT WOULD THEY SAY?

Sometime you may get a chance to have the young women communicate a few things to you. Bishop H. David Burton, the presiding bishop of the Church, had an interesting conversation with his sixteen-year-old granddaughter, a Laurel.

I asked her what she would tell the young men of the Aaronic Priesthood if she could speak to them. She said, "Grandpa, I would ask them to show respect for the priesthood and to be priesthood holders seven days a week rather than just one day, Sunday. Some guys do not show respect for the priesthood because they use profanity; some are involved in pornography; and a few are into drugs." I'm certain, my young brethren, that you'll agree that profanity, pornography, and drugs should not be a part of the life of a priesthood holder ("Honoring the Priesthood," *Ensign,* May 2000, 39).

If you ever have the chance to help plan an activity in your ward, it might be fun to ask the young women for their input. And while you're at it, ask them for ideas on how you could honor your priesthood. You could also strengthen the young women by sharing your feelings about how they could honor their young womanhood.

DON'T LET THE YOUNG WOMEN READ THIS PART (ON SECOND THOUGHT, MAKE THEM READ IT)

I'm going to mention what follows because I've had more than a few young men mention this to me. Some girls seem interested only in the guys who are popular or athletic. Oddly enough, others seem interested only in young men who are arrogant and crude, and who don't treat young women with much respect. They say that girls mature faster than boys, but when I witness that kind of behavior, I think it's a debatable point. I've seen some really nice girls go for some pretty unimpressive guys.

If you have seen this, don't let it bother you, and don't lower your behavior to be like second-class guys. Someday, those *girls* will become *women* who will realize that the young men who truly honor their priesthood make the best husbands. Who do you think the young women would rather spend their lives with? A popular guy who used to be a varsity-class jock or a priesthood holder who is a world-class husband?

If it bothers you that only a certain group of boys seem to get the attention of all the girls, be patient. The girls will grow up, and so will you. (If it still bothers you, just imagine some Saturday night way in the future. Some of those girls will be bored out of their minds while their husbands are in the living room, glued to ESPN, chewing on a microwaved burrito, and hollering about the lost remote.

Meanwhile, *your* wife will be swooning and grinning from ear to ear as she looks out the window and watches you and the boys climb in the van and drive off to general priesthood meeting.)

Yes, some young women can have their attention temporarily diverted by athletes and automobiles, but be patient and keep the faith. You're not looking for a wife until after your mission anyway. Your future wife will be there when you get home. And, I surmise, that those who are wise will recognize the honorable guys—(please pass the fries).

If you happen to be a high school athlete, good for you. You can be the rarest kind—one who honors his priesthood and respects young women. And you can be an example to every person at your school—students, coaches, and teachers. Then you can properly be called an *athlete,* not just a jock (there's a difference). President Gordon B. Hinckley counseled the young men:

 I do not want you to be self-righteous. I want you to be manly, to be vibrant and strong and happy. To those who are athletically inclined, I want you to be good athletes and strive to become champions. But in

doing so, you do not have to indulge in unseemly behavior or profane and filthy language" ("Personal Worthiness to Exercise the Priesthood," *Ensign,* May 2002, 53).

OH, BROTHER . . .

As a priesthood holder in your family, you can influence your siblings and even your parents by honoring your priesthood. You will probably attend the same school with your brothers and sisters, and in some ways, you will be better acquainted than your parents with what your siblings go through. Your opinion will matter to your sister. Elder Richard G. Scott said:

> As a brother, you can have a powerful, positive influence in your sister's life. Compliment her when she looks especially nice. She may listen to you more than to your parents when you suggest that she wear modest clothing. Simple courtesies like opening the door for her and building her self-esteem will encourage her to find her real worth ("The Sanctity of Womanhood," *Ensign,* May 2000, 37).

When you were a child, your family's job was to take care of you and teach you. Now that you're a young man, your job is to help take care of your family and teach your younger siblings by your example. You can't criticize everyone and everything and still honor your priesthood. You can't just consume milk and cereal and produce dirty laundry and not give anything back. The Lord expects more of you, and the priesthood requires it. If you complain about family home evening, family scripture study, and family prayer, you're not honoring your priesthood. You can help your family members in their spiritual progress rather than just parking on the couch and muttering, "That's my parents' job." President Ezra Taft Benson says that running a family is your job too:

> Young men, the family unit is forever, and you should do everything in your power to strengthen that unit. In your own family, encourage family home evenings and be an active participant. Encourage family prayer and be on your knees with your family in that sacred circle. Do your part to develop real family unity and solidarity. In such homes, there is no generation gap. Your most important friendships should be with your own brothers and sisters and with your father and mother. Love your family. Be loyal to them. Have a

genuine concern for your brothers and sisters. Help carry their load so you can say, like the lyrics of that song, "He ain't heavy; he's my brother." Remember, the family is one of God's greatest fortresses against the evils of our day. Help keep your family strong and close and worthy of our Father in Heaven's blessings. As you do, you will receive faith and strength which will bless your lives forever ("To the 'Youth of the Noble Birthright,'" *Ensign,* May 1986, 43).

If you will do these things, your mother and father will look at each other and say, "Who is this kid?" And they'll thank their Father in Heaven for you at the close of each day. As you learned from the beginning of this book, you are not average, and you can't afford to act that way. Instead, you have been called to be peculiar, called to hold a royal priesthood and to let your light shine to the world.

Graduate with Honor

One of the greatest things you can achieve in junior high and high school is not popularity or even good grades. It's the respect of your classmates. Everyone knows what respect is, but not everyone knows how to get it. You do. As you honor your priesthood, you have the perfect formula for earning respect from your peers. You respect yourself by not drinking, partying, using drugs, and viewing pornographic entertainment. You respect others by using clean, classy language, and by always building up those around you. And you respect young women because you see them as your spirit sisters, or as daughters of God, whose honor and virtue ought to be defended and protected.

Do these things, and others will respect you. They'll see something different in you that they'll admire. They'll notice that you're self-assured but never self-righteous. And they'll remember that respect long after graduation day.

At one time I attended a ward which had almost no Melchizedek Priesthood holders in it. But it was not in any way dulled in spirituality. On the contrary, many of its members witnessed the greatest display of priesthood power they had ever known.

The power was centered in the priests. For the first time in their lives they were called upon to perform all the duties of the priests and administer to the needs of their fellow ward members. They were seriously called to home teach—not just to be a yawning appendage to an elder making a social call but to bless their brothers and sisters.

Previous to this time I had been with four of these priests in a different situation. There I regarded them to be common hood-lums. They drove away every seminary teacher after two or three months. They spread havoc over the countryside on Scouting trips. But when they were needed—when they were trusted with a vital mission—they were among those who shone the most brilliantly in priesthood service.

The secret was that the bishop called upon his Aaronic Priesthood to rise to the stature of men to whom angels might well appear; and they rose to that stature, administering relief to those who might be in want and strengthening those who needed strengthening. Not only were the other ward members built up but so were the members of the quorum themselves. A great unity spread throughout the ward and every member began to have a taste of what it is for a people to be of one mind and one heart. There was nothing inexplicable in all of this; it was just the proper exercise of the Aaronic Priesthood (Cited by Victor L. Brown in "The Vision of the Aaronic Priesthood," Ensign, *November 1975, 68).*

12

Home Teaching—More Than Just Sitting on a Couch

Too often the young men of the Church say things like this:

• A service project? Why can't we do something fun?

• Is youth conference just going to be a bunch of classes? Why can't we go somewhere?

• Another meeting? Are we gonna have refreshments?

• Why do we always have to dress up?

• If this is boring, I'm going home.

• Home teaching? Do I have to say anything?

Unlike you, the young men who say such things haven't quite caught the vision, have they? Oh well, give them time and they'll grow up. Maybe adults have to share a portion of the blame. Sometimes adult leaders sell the young people short by assuming that they must be constantly enter- tained or served. The priesthood is about serving, not getting served. President Joseph Fielding Smith said, "It is a mistake for us to draw within ourselves as does a snail into its shell. No man has been given the Priesthood as an ornament only. He is expected to use it in behalf of the salvation of others" (*The Way to Perfection* [Salt Lake City: Deseret Book, 1975], 218).

One of the ways we serve is as a home teacher. Your home teaching service begins when you are a teacher and continues throughout your life. Moroni spoke of some form of home teaching back in 400 A.D. Listen to him explain what happens to new members after baptism:

"And after they had been received unto baptism, and were wrought upon and cleansed by the power of the Holy Ghost, they were numbered among the people of the church of Christ; and their names were taken, that they might be remembered and nourished by the good word of God, to keep them in the right way, to keep them continually watchful unto prayer, relying alone upon the merits of Christ, who was the author and the finisher of their faith" (Moroni 6:4).

"Numbered among the people of the church of Christ; and their names were taken." They made a record! They kept roll! Why would they do that?

"That they might be remembered." Nobody wants to be forgotten, and the Lord requires the Church to remember people and to care for them and love them. That's where home teachers come in! We help the bishop by letting all members know they are important, and that they will not be forgotten.

"And nourished by the good word of God." When we share our home teaching message and our testimonies, we give the spirit of the Lord the opportunity to warm the hearts of those we visit.

"To keep them in the right way." Home teachers can ask family members how they're doing and if they need any help. Home teachers can remind them of their baptismal covenants and of their opportunity to attend church and renew their covenants.

"To keep them continually watchful unto prayer." Home teachers can pray with the family and encourage the family to hold regular family prayer.

"Relying alone upon the merits of Christ."
Jesus Christ is the head of the Church. Home teachers can make the Savior the heart of their message. He is our only hope for salvation and peace in this life, and the foundation of our faith.

I can't think of a better scripture to explain why we have home teachers than Moroni 6:4. But what if you're just a kid? What if you're only fourteen or fifteen or sixteen or seventeen? Do you really have to ask the father of your families if he's having family prayer? What if the person you home teach is the bishop or the stake president? What if he's a general authority? Or the prophet? I'm glad you asked.

So, President Smith, Are You Saying Your Prayers?

This is the story of a seventeen-year-old named William Cahoon, who was assigned to be the home teacher, or "ward teacher" back then, to Joseph Smith!

> I was called and ordained to act as a teacher to visit the families of the Saints. I got along very well till I found that I was obliged to call and pay a visit to the Prophet. Being young, only about seventeen

years of age, I felt my weakness in visiting the
Prophet and his family in the capacity of a teacher.
I almost felt like shrinking from duty. Finally I
went to his door and knocked, and in a minute the

Prophet came to the door. I stood there trembling, and said to him, "Brother Joseph, I have come to visit you in the capacity of a teacher, if it is convenient for you."

He said, "Brother William, come right in, I am glad to see you; sit down in that chair there and I will go and call my family in."

They soon came in and took seats. He then said, "Brother William, I submit myself and family into your hands."

He then took his seat. "Now Brother William," said he, "ask all the questions you feel like."

By this time all my fears and trembling had ceased, and I said, "Brother Joseph, are you trying to live your religion?"

He answered, "Yes."

I then said, "Do you pray in your family?"

He said, "Yes."

"Do you teach your family the principles of the gospel?"

He replied, "Yes, I am trying to do it."

"Do you ask a blessing on your food?"

He answered, "Yes."

"Are you trying to live in peace and harmony with all your family?"

He said that he was.

I then turned to Sister Emma, his wife, and said,

"Sister Emma, are you trying to live your religion? Do you teach your children to obey their parents? Do you try to teach them to pray?"

To all these questions she answered, "Yes, I am trying to do so."

I then turned to Joseph and said, "I am now through with my questions as a teacher; and now if you have any instructions to give, I shall be happy to receive them."

He said, "God bless you, Brother William; and if you are humble and faithful, you shall have power to settle all difficulties that may come before you in the capacity of a teacher."

As a teacher, I then left my parting blessing upon him and his family and took my departure (Joseph Smith, *Encyclopedia of Joseph Smith's Teachings,* ed. Larry E. Dahl and Donald Q. Cannon [Salt Lake City: Deseret Book, 2000], 324–25).

Can you imagine asking those questions of the prophet? Brother Cahoon asked them because that's what he was called to do. So don't worry about your age, worry about your duty! President Harold B. Lee taught:

When you ask a teacher what are his duties, he may answer, "Well, it's to do home teaching." But you may wish to say to him, "When you do home teaching you are representing the Lord, to visit the home of each member, to see that they are doing their duty, and to see that they are all keeping the commandments of God" (Conference Report, April 1969, 23).

Home teaching is terrific preparation for a mission. You go with a companion, you knock on doors, you go inside, you sit down, you teach, and you try to deliver a spiritual message.

If I could live my Aaronic Priesthood years over again, I would watch my senior companion very carefully. I would notice what he says, when he sits down, how he sits when he teaches, what he talks about, and what he says. I would ask him to let me present the lesson every once in a while too. I would refuse to simply be a "yawning appendage" to my senior companion.

The Church of Jesus Christ of Latter-day Saints isn't the kind of church in which you can just lock yourself in a castle and read the scriptures and pray to be holy. This church is about helping others. When Jesus was asked what the greatest commandment was, he responded, "Thou shalt love the Lord thy God with all thy heart, and with all thy soul, and with all thy mind," and "Thou shalt love thy neighbor as thyself" (Matthew 22:38–39).

I used to think that being spiritual meant you knew a lot. I was wrong. Being spiritual isn't just about knowing things. It's about knowing things and doing something about what you know. The Lord isn't as concerned about what we know as he is about what we are becoming. When we serve and look out for each other, when we truly love our neighbor, we become something different than we were before.

Young men who are becoming something can often be overheard to say such things as

- A service project? Those are fun. When is it?
- Youth conference is at the stake center this year? Yeah, I'm going.
- Another meeting? Uh-huh, I'll be there. I might learn something.
- Mom, where's my dress shirt? I gotta go to church.
- I refuse to be bored. How can I make this better?
- Home teaching? Can I teach the lesson this time?

ONWARD WITH HONOR

PRESIDENT GORDON B. HINCKLEY:

"You are not 'dead-end' kids. You are not wasting your lives in drifting aimlessly. You have purpose. You have design. You have plans that can only lead to growth and strength. When your energies are harnessed, when your dreams are focused, marvelous things happen" ("To the Boys and to the Men," *Ensign,* November 1998, 51).

BISHOP VICTOR L. BROWN:

"You priests in the Aaronic Priesthood are of a royal generation. You are sons of God with great power and unlimited potential. You have been in training for the past five or six years in preparation for the greatest honor and responsibility that comes to man, and that is the Melchizedek Priesthood— the power to act in the name of God and have your actions ratified in the heavens. In the process of your training, you have been taught by presiding officers, particularly your bishop who is president of your quorum. He has given you instruction with regard to the sacrament service and baptism and your responsibility for home teaching. . . . He has taught you how your appearance and cleanliness both externally and internally are so important if you are to be a proper example to others" ("The Role of the Priest," *New Era,* May 1974, 12).

PRESIDENT WILFORD WOODRUFF:

"I went out as a Priest, and my companion as an Elder, and we traveled thousands of miles, and had many things manifested to us. I desire to impress upon you the fact that it does not make any difference whether a man is a Priest or an Apostle, if he magnifies his calling. A Priest holds the keys of the ministering of angels. Never in my life, as an Apostle, as a Seventy, or as an Elder, have I ever had more of the protection of the Lord than while holding the office of Priest" (in the *Millennial Star,* 5 October 1891, 628–29).

BISHOP H. BURKE PETERSON:

"Brethren, let's consider again why we cannot be involved in Satan's program of entertainment and be held guiltless. Why? Because *we are men and boys of the covenant,* and that makes us different from all others. When we've made a covenant with the

Lord, we are special—not ordinary, but special. He loves all of his sons, *but those of the covenant have a special responsibility*" ("'Touch Not the Evil Gift, Nor the Unclean Thing,'" *Ensign,* November 1993, 42).

13

Preparing for the Melchizedek Priesthood

In ten years, you will be somewhere. The question is, where?

In ten years, you will have become something. The question is, what?

Your future is in your hands. You will become what your thoughts, actions, and decisions have made you during your Aaronic Priesthood years. The Aaronic Priesthood is the finest training available to help you meet your future challenges and responsibilities. In fact, if you will take full advantage of the opportunities you have in the Aaronic Priesthood, in scouting, in seminary, and in magnifying your callings, you will be able to perform miracles throughout your life. President Ezra Taft Benson explained how your past behavior can create a miraculous future:

Give me a young man who has kept himself morally clean and has faithfully attended his Church meetings. Give me a young man who has magnified his priesthood and has earned the Duty to God Award and is an Eagle Scout. Give me a young man who is a seminary graduate and has a burning testimony of the Book of Mormon. Give me such a young man, and I will give you a young man who can perform miracles for the Lord in the mission field and throughout his life ("To the 'Youth of the Noble Birthright,'" *Ensign,* May 1986, 45).

Let's take a look at the formula President Benson outlined:

"Give me a young man who has kept himself morally clean." We've already covered a little bit about the addictive nature of pornography and about respecting young women, but let's talk about dating. Those of you who are priests are old enough to drive and date. These are privileges. Whenever a privilege is given, responsibility is also given. When you earn the privilege to drive a car, your responsibility is to learn to obey the rules of the road. Also, when you start the car and leave the driveway, you need to have a destination in mind.

The Lord and his servants have outlined the rules of the road when it comes to dating, and the gospel supplies us with our destination. Your destination, as a priest in the Aaronic Priesthood, is a full-time mission. Therefore, your purpose in dating should be to develop friendships and social skills. Anything that might keep you from reaching your destination is a roadblock that will also keep you from achieving your full potential as a son of God.

Young women who are wise will want you to serve a mission. They know that a mission is like a "shortcut to maturity." A mission will prepare you to be a better husband and father, and it will teach you things about people and the gospel that you couldn't possibly learn by staying home. What are the rules of the road concerning dating? Here are some guidelines from *For the Strength of Youth:*

• "Date only those who have high standards and in whose company you can maintain your standards."

• "Do not date until you are at least sixteen years old."

• "Go in groups or on double dates. Avoid going on frequent dates with the same person" (*For the Strength of Youth: Fulfilling Our Duty to God* [Salt

Lake City: The Church of Jesus Christ of Latter-day Saints, 2001], 24).

If your dating is getting too serious and taking you away from your destination of a full-time mission, you'd better find a rest stop and review the rules of the road. Satan wants to convince you that everyone else is going down forbidden paths. Why can't you follow? Because Satan's paths lead to nothing but dark, disappointing, dead-ends. *For the Strength of Youth* talks about some of those forbidden roads concerning your behavior on dates:

> Before marriage, do not do anything to arouse the powerful emotions that must be expressed only in marriage. Do not participate in passionate kissing, lie on top of another person, or touch the private, sacred parts of another person's body, with or without clothing. Do not allow anyone to do that with you. Do not arouse those emotions in your own body (*For the Strength of Youth*, 27).

As a priest preparing for a mission, you should read the entire sections on "Dating" and "Sexual Purity" in your *For the Strength of Youth* booklet. Keep in mind that this booklet could have been named *How to Reach Your Maximum Potential, How to Enjoy Maximum Happiness,* or even *How Not to Mess Up Your Life.*

The booklet is not just a bunch of rules designed to make sure you don't have any fun. I am convinced that each paragraph was carefully written, pored over, and prayed about. The Lord and his servants want you to reach all your goals and fulfill all that you were foreordained to do. Remember, the young woman you're going to marry is out there somewhere. Elder Gerald N. Lund taught:

> When I was sixteen years old and not smart enough to know very much at all, the Spirit touched my heart and I realized the significance of the woman that you marry. Starting at that time I began to pray that the Lord would find for me the woman who would be my eternal companion. Those prayers were answered ("The Opportunity to Serve," *Ensign,* May 2002, 85).

If all Aaronic Priesthood holders of dating age could sense the seriousness of their future marriage, they would never think of the dating standards the same way again. And they would never feel restricted by the standards. Think about it. Your future wife is out there. She wants you to be amazing. Honor your priesthood by being morally clean, not just for you but also for her! Live up to everything she wants you to be.

"Give me a young man who has . . . faithfully attended his church meetings." One of the greatest keys to success, and one of the greatest keys to honoring your priesthood, is to be where you are supposed to be. Each Sunday, you have the chance to be with people who believe the things you believe. You have the chance to learn and strengthen each other, and most important, you have the chance to renew your baptismal covenants while helping others do the same!

Someone once said that going to church doesn't make you a Christian any more than sleeping in the garage makes you a Chevrolet. That's true. But when you go to church, and when you actually go to class instead of lingering in the foyer or sitting on the couch, you might just learn the gospel line upon line, precept upon precept. Week by week, month by month, you learn the doctrines that you will eventually teach to others on your mission. And when we actually "take what the teacher says into our daily lives," as we often say in prayer, we might actually become Christians.

When you go to church weekly, you renew your baptismal covenants. You have a fresh chance each week to start again with a clean slate. When you renew your promise to keep the commandments, the Lord renews his promise that you will always have his spirit to be with you. That spirit will help you make crucial decisions that lie ahead.

"Give me a young man who has . . . magnified his priesthood." One of my favorite toys as a young man was my Dad's binoculars. I don't think Dad considered his binoculars one of my toys, but I did. His "binos" made small things bigger. President Gordon B. Hinckley used binoculars to explain what it means to magnify the priesthood.

> All of you, of course, are familiar with binoculars. When you put the lenses to your eyes and focus them, you magnify and in effect bring closer all within your field of vision. But if you turn them around and look through the other end, you diminish and make more distant that which you see.
>
> So it is with our actions as holders of the priesthood. When we live up to our high and holy calling, when we show love for God through service to fellowmen, when we use our strength and

talents to build faith and spread truth, we magnify our priesthood. When, on the other hand, we live lives of selfishness, when we indulge in sin, when we set our sights only on the things of the world rather than on the things of God, we diminish our priesthood ("Magnify Your Calling," *Ensign,* May 1989, 47).

To magnify our priesthood is to fulfill our responsibilities and to complete our assignments willingly. One of the great blessings you have as a bearer of the Aaronic Priesthood is inspired leadership. You don't have to figure out everything alone. As a deacon, teacher, or priest, you have a quorum adviser. As you advance in the Aaronic Priesthood, watch your advisers carefully and ask them lots of questions. Your leaders can help you find ways to magnify your priesthood in your ward.

"Give me a young man who . . . has earned the Duty to God award and is an Eagle Scout." Some of the best memories of my young life involved scouting and the Aaronic Priesthood. I remember several of us lying in our sleeping bags while one of our leaders, Dwight Matheson, stood in the middle of the tent and told us thrilling war stories from the Book of Mormon. Since we were all sitting in a tent, he told us about Teancum and how he snuck into tents (Alma 51:33–35). Up until that time, I didn't realize that there were such cool things in the Book of Mormon!

I remember a scout meeting in which Earl Shepherd patiently outlined the entire "Citizenship in the World" merit badge on a chalkboard. I also remember that we were pretty rowdy that night. I felt bad, so I went home and worked on the merit badge until I earned it.

I remember sitting in Sunday School while Cal Hardman taught us about the goodness of God, and how truth and goodness will always prevail. That day still sticks out in my memory because during that lesson my attention was glued to Brother Hardman, instead of to the girls we sat with. I knew that he had a testimony, and it showed.

Mostly, I remember going to church week after week and preparing the sacrament so that everyone in my ward could renew their covenants with the Lord. Why have I shared this? Because none of these experiences would have been mine if I had not gone to Church! I am grateful for all that I achieved in scouting and in high school. But if I had to pick my most important achievement as a young man, it would definitely be my Duty to God award. Today I can show you my Duty to God award because I showed up at church each week.

But your Duty to God medal is not just an award—it's a way of life. Your duty to God doesn't end once your mother pins the medal on your scout shirt. Your duty is just beginning. It will continue on your mission and throughout the rest of your life. The award doesn't mean you're done doing your duty to God but rather that you've learned what your duty to God is.

You've learned the daily habits of prayer and scripture study. You've learned to strive to keep the commandments and attend your meetings. You've learned that service to your fellow beings is what God expects. You've learned that life is all about giving and serving, not just getting and "vegging." You've learned to live the words of the hymn, "Because I have been given much, I too must give" (*Hymns,* 1985, no. 219).

Now that you know your duty, you must do it. It's nice to know what to do, but now you must do what you know. Doing your duty will help you to become someone extraordinary. Your duty to God is to give your life to God. And in doing so, you don't lose anything. President Ezra Taft Benson taught that when we give our lives to God, he gives us much more in return!

Men and women who turn their lives over to God will discover that He can make a lot more out of their lives than they can. He will deepen their joys, expand their vision, quicken their minds, strengthen their muscles, lift their spirits, multiply their blessings, increase their opportunities, comfort their souls, raise up friends, and pour out peace. Whoever will lose his life in the service of God will find eternal life ("Jesus Christ—Gifts and Expectations," *New Era,* May 1975, 20; emphasis added).

The Boy Scout motto is "Be Prepared." Your Duty to God medal signifies spiritual preparation for a lifetime of service to your Heavenly Father.

"Give me a young man who is a seminary graduate and has a burning testimony of the Book of Mormon." It took me a long time to realize what a blessing it was to go to seminary. What if every teenager on earth were to take an hour a day and study the teachings of Jesus Christ? What would happen to gangs? Drugs? War? Hatred?

Racism? Crime? What if all of us tried to pattern our lives after the Prince of Peace? It would be a different world. President Gordon B. Hinckley taught:

> Now, I'd like to say just a word to the young people here, you who are in your teens, you wonderful hope of the future, you faithful young Latter-day Saints, you who attend seminary and go to institute, you who are the best generation we have ever had in this Church: Be faithful. Be true. Don't let yourselves fall into evil ways. Take advantage of your great opportunities. Get all of the education you can possibly get. Education is the key which will unlock the door of opportunity, and the Lord has laid upon you the responsibility to secure an education ("Inspirational Thoughts," *Ensign,* July 1998, 4).

"Give me such a young man, and I will give you a young man who can perform miracles for the Lord in the mission field and throughout his life." What will these miracles be? What will you achieve on your mission? Young men, the best is yet to come! Your future is yet to be written. The rest of your life is a large volume of empty pages to

be completed by you. No one else can compose the pages of your life. You hold the pen in your hand. President Thomas S. Monson said:

Remember, my young friends, you are somebody! You are a child of promise. You are a man of might. You are a son of God, endowed with faith, gifted with courage, and guided by prayer. Your eternal destiny is before you. The Apostle Paul speaks to you today as he spoke to Timothy long years ago: "Neglect not the gift that is in thee. . . . O Timothy, keep that which is committed to thy trust" (1 Timothy 4:14; 1 Timothy 6:20).

As you define your goals and plan for their achievement, ponder the thought: The past is behind—learn from it; the future is ahead—prepare for it; the present is here—live in it ("Go For It!" *Ensign,* May 1989, 43).

Conclusion

Elder M. Russell Ballard taught:

No young man should aspire to a calling, but as surely as you are sitting in this priesthood meeting tonight, many of you will preside over wards, stakes, missions, quorums, and, of course, your own families. Priesthood training, my brethren, starts when a young man is ordained a deacon in the Aaronic Priesthood. You Aaronic Priesthood bearers need to understand that you are in training. . . . Train hard. Get ready. The Church needs you.

The world needs you. The Lord needs you ("Prepare to Serve," *Ensign,* May 1985, 41, 43).

What is the priesthood? It is the power of God delegated to man to act in all things for the salvation of man. Where did you get it? The priesthood of God has been on the earth since the beginning. Aaron, the brother of Moses (and a member of the tribe of Levi) held it, and it was passed on through generations and held by John the Baptist. On May 15, 1829, John the Baptist appeared and restored it to Joseph Smith and Oliver Cowdery. It has been passed down through the generations until it was conferred upon you. What will you do with it? You will serve! You will serve the Church by administering the outward ordinances of baptism and the sacrament of the Lord's supper.

How will you honor the priesthood? By keeping the covenants you made at baptism. By standing as a witness of God at all times, in all things, and in all places. You will honor it by dressing in a way that shows respect for who you are, by carefully controlling what you see and hear, and by controlling your tongue and your thoughts. You will honor the priesthood by showing respect for young women and by fulfilling your responsibilities to bless the lives of others, whether or not they are members of the Church.

As brothers in the priesthood, I honor you. I honor you for reading this book all the way to the end. I honor you for wanting to know who you are and for wanting to do your duty. I honor you for being young men who will change the world.

Index